The Essence of Business Economics

Joseph G. Nellis
Senior Lecturer in Business Economics
Cranfield School of Management

and

David Parker
Senior Lecturer in Business Economics
Cranfield School of Management

Prentice Hall

New York   London   Toronto   Sydney   Tokyo   Singapore

First published 1992 by
Prentice Hall International (UK) Ltd
Campus 400, Maylands Avenue
Hemel Hempstead
Hertfordshire, HP2 7EZ
A division of
Simon & Schuster International Group

© Prentice Hall International (UK) Ltd, 1992

Typeset in 10/12 pt Palatino
by Keyset Composition, Colchester, Essex

Printed and bound in Great Britain by
Redwood Books Limited, Trowbridge, Wiltshire

Library of Congress Cataloging-in-Publication Data

Nellis, J. G.
    The essence of business economics / Joseph G. Nellis and David
Parker.
        p.   cm. -- (The Essence of management series)
    Includes bibliographical references and index.
    ISBN 0-13-284761-2 (pbk)
    1. Managerial economics. I. Parker, David, 1949– . II. Title.
III. Series
    HD30.22.N45   1992
    338.5'024658--dc20

92-12062
CIP

British Library Cataloguing in Publication Data

A catalogue record for this book is available from
the British Library

ISBN 0-13-284761-2 (pbk)

4   5   96   95

To
Helen, Gareth, Daniel and Kathleen
Megan, Michael and Matthew

Contents

Preface

This book is not intended to create economists. Managers are not economists, nor need they be. Instead, it is intended to introduce managers and trainee managers to the essence of business economics; to those concepts, theories and ideas which form the economist's tool kit. The rationale for the book lies in a belief that, armed with an understanding of business economics, managers can understand and hence better react to changes in the competitive environment in which their businesses operate. Since business economics is a compulsory element of many professional management training courses, the book will be particularly useful for those studying on Master of Business Administration (MBA) and Diploma in Management (DMS) programmes as well as practising managers attending continuing studies courses in which business economics is an integral part. In addition, the book is also suitably structured for students attending business studies and general economics courses at universities, polytechnics and colleges of further and higher education.

In particular, the book studies the nature of consumer demand and costs of production within different types of competitive markets. Factors impacting on demand are considered and methods for forecasting demand are investigated, while the behaviour of costs over time and as output changes is studied in detail. The book contains a review of the various business objectives management might pursue and their differing implications for optimal pricing and investment policies. It also surveys the impact of government on the environment in which the firm ultimately thrives or dies and discusses in particular the nature of industrial, competition and regional policies. There is a brief introduction to macroeconomic policy and more specifically demand management, though readers requiring a more detailed treatment of this subject are directed to our companion volume in this series, *The Essence of the Economy*.

We are once again indebted to Christine Williams who has stoically dealt with the typing and retyping of the various and often almost illegible drafts of this book. We would like to acknowledge the patience and encouragement of Cathy Peck of Prentice Hall; it is no easy task to manage two independently minded authors who always promise completion of a manuscript 'tomorrow'! Our thanks also go to our MBA students at the Cranfield School of Management. They have helped to create a uniquely challenging environment for us as lecturers and authors and we owe a great deal to them. Their constant questioning has proved invaluable in focusing our ideas. We would also like to acknowledge the support of our colleagues and notably our friend Dr Frank Fishwick. Frank has that rare quality of posing the questions that no one else appears to have thought about!

Lastly, of course, the greatest tribute must be to our wives and children who have once again borne the sacrifice to family life, which results from writing, with their usual cheerfulness.

Joseph G. Nellis
David Parker
Cranfield School of Management

1

The essence of business economics: an overview

The essence of business economics

Today, the economic, political and social environments are changing faster than ever before. Business success depends, therefore, on managers anticipating and coping with change. To do this managers must first identify the characteristics of the world in which they operate. That 'world' may be examined at the following two levels:

- **The microeconomic environment.**
- **The macroeconomic environment.**

The microeconomic environment deals with the operation of the firm in its immediate market, involving the determination of prices, revenues, costs, employment levels and so on. In contrast, the macroeconomic environment comprises the general social and economic conditions of the larger system of which each firm forms a part. This larger system involves the impact of political, legal and economic decisions, both nationally and internationally. By definition, since any single firm usually represents a minute part of the larger system, it is unlikely to be able to exercise control over the macroeconomic environment in the way in which it may be able to have control over its microeconomic environment (as in the case of a monopoly firm, for example).

The macroeconomic environment is covered in our companion

volume to this series entitled *The Essence of the Economy*. In terms of Figure 1.1, this book dealt with the impact of the wider international and domestic economies on the firm; whereas the current book is solely concerned with a study of the immediate environment of the firm, i.e. business economics.

Our aim here is to meet the needs of the manager in the daily process of decision-making. Decisions, if they are to be effective, must be soundly based on a critical awareness of the fundamental economic relationships which underlie all business operations. The manager must be able to apply this understanding and knowledge to real-world problems. An understanding of the key concepts of business economics provides a sound foundation for optimal decision-making. The subjects of marketing, strategic management, finance and so on, utilize many of the core concepts introduced here.

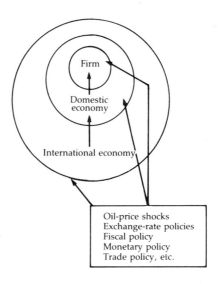

Figure 1.1   The business environment

Basic concepts in business economics

There are a number of basic concepts which lie at the heart of business economics and managerial decision-making. The most important of these are the following:

- Resource allocation.
- Opportunity cost.
- Diminishing marginal returns.
- Marginal analysis.
- Business objectives.
- Time dimension.
- Externalities.
- Discounting.

We start by briefly describing the relevance of each of these to business economics.

Resource allocation

When purchasing raw materials, employing labour and undertaking investment, the manager is involved in *resource allocation*. Society's resources are, inevitably, scarce so that the individual firm has to pay for them. Decisions need to be made at three levels, namely:

- **what** goods and services to produce with the available resources;
- **how** to combine the available resources to produce different types of goods and services, and
- **for whom** the different goods and services are to be supplied.

Figure 1.2 illustrates the interrelationship between the production decision and decisions regarding these three factors. Such decisions are sometimes described as the *allocative, productive* and *distributive* choices respectively which face society in general. In business economics we examine how the price mechanism relates to making these choices.

Traditionally, the price mechanism has been seen as the major determinant of the *what, how* and *for whom* decisions, especially in

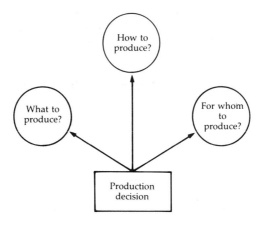

Figure 1.2   The production decision

market economies, though less so in the formerly centrally planned or command economies of Eastern Europe. However, over time in all economies firms have grown in size and importance – witness for example resource allocation which goes on *within* companies such as IBM, ICI and Toyota. Resources within firms are allocated by both command and price. For example, a decision on where to locate plant could be based upon detailed costings of alternative sites (price). Alternatively, the decision might be made by management on the basis of non-price factors, which may in fact be purely subjective ('a nice area of the country to live').

In so far as resource allocation in firms results from command rather than price, as Professor Robertson observed, firms might be considered to be 'islands of conscious power in . . . [an] ocean of unconscious co-operation' (Robertson and Dennison, 1960). The market therefore represents a network of unconscious co-operation between a multitude of buyers and sellers. At the same time, the boundary between the firm and the market is constantly evolving through mergers, takeovers, divestment, management buyouts, etc. Firms are constantly reassessing their structures and strategies and attempting to answer questions such as whether or not they should undertake in-house those activities which are currently purchased in the market (e.g. take over a supplier?), or, instead, should certain activities which are currently undertaken and purchased in the market (e.g. software development in the case of a computer manufacturer) be closed down or sold off?

The so-called 'make or buy' decision needs to be constantly monitored. The American economist Oliver Williamson has referred to this as a decision about the *boundary of the firm*. Where is the boundary of the firm to be drawn? In other words, what activities should be directed by the 'conscious power' of management and what should be the prerogative of the 'unconscious co-operation' which is the hallmark of the market? The firm or the market is a choice between the allocation of resources in 'markets' or 'hierarchies'. Sometimes it will pay to buy in the market while sometimes it will be more efficient to undertake an activity in-house. In economic terms, the deciding factor will be relative costs. The manager, therefore, needs to be aware of not only the current costs of production but also the costs of the alternative method of supply. This brings us to the economist's concept of *opportunity cost*.

Opportunity cost

Underlying business decisions is the fact that resources are scarce. This scarcity can be reflected in many ways, such as shortages of capital, physical and human resources, and time. The existence of scarcity means that whenever a decision or choice is made, a cost is incurred. Economists take a broader view of such a cost than that based purely on monetary factors as used by accountants. In economists' jargon, such costs include opportunity costs.

The opportunity cost of any activity is the loss of the opportunity to pursue the most attractive alternative given the same time and resources.

The concept of opportunity cost can be usefully illustrated using a simple diagram. In Figure 1.3, the curve PP represents what is called a *production possibility curve* (PPC).

A production possibility curve shows the maximum output of two goods or services that can be produced given the current level of resources available and assuming maximum efficiency in production.

Any firm with its available *factors of production* (which may be broadly categorized as land, labour and capital) has a choice as to the products it may produce. For example, suppose that a business school runs both an MBA programme and continuing studies courses for practising managers. It is able to provide either 0A places for MBA students or 0B places for practising managers or some combination of both shown along the PP curve. Now suppose that

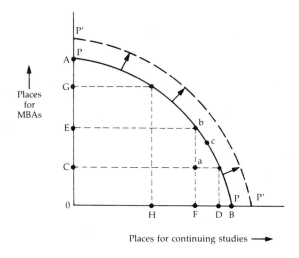

Figure 1.3   Production possibility curve

currently the business school provides 0C MBA places and 0D continuing studies places, but decides to expand its MBA provision to 0E. Given current resources, these extra MBA places can only be achieved by reducing the continuing studies activities to 0F. In other words, the opportunity cost of accommodating CE extra MBA students is DF fewer continuing studies places. Similar trade-offs between the two activities are shown along the PP curve. The *shape* of the curve reflects the fact that in business, as resources are transferred from one activity to another, the resulting increase in activity (in this case MBA places) is likely to decline. This relates to the concept of *diminishing marginal returns*.

Diminishing marginal returns

The concept of diminishing marginal returns refers to the situation whereby as we apply more of one input (e.g. labour) to another input (e.g. capital or land), then after some point the resulting increase in output becomes smaller and smaller.

For example, in the case of the business school, the transfer of equal amounts of resources from continuing studies courses to MBA provision may produce an increasingly smaller addition to the MBA output if MBA teaching requires higher-level skills than continuing studies teaching. If the business school continues to increase its MBA numbers by a given amount, it is likely to have to reduce its continuing studies places by a proportionately greater amount. For example, returning to Figure 1.3, an increase in the number of MBA students of EG (where EG = CE) leads to a fall in continuing studies places of FH. As will be appreciated from the diagram, FH is greater than DF.

Of course, if the business school had *not* been using its resources to maximum efficiency then it could have increased the number of MBA students without cutting its continuing studies courses by simply becoming more efficient (in Figure 1.3 this is shown by moving from point a, below the PP curve, to point b on the curve). Equally, it could have increased provision of *both* courses by moving to, for example, point c. To increase provision beyond the PP curve (as shown by P'P') naturally requires more resources, e.g. lecture rooms, lecturers, etc. These sorts of choices and hence the issue of resource allocation lie at the heart of business decision-making.

Marginal analysis

The idea of opportunity cost highlights that choices have to be made regarding what to produce. The concept of *the margin* reminds us that most of these choices involve relatively small (incremental) increases or decreases in production. For example, decisions have to be made regarding whether to provide an extra MBA class, an extra production shift, to generate an extra megawatt of electricity, to produce 1,000 fewer ball-bearings, to add a product to the product range, etc. Only relatively rarely do we make decisions about all or nothing, e.g. whether to be a manufacturer or not! The scale of the increase or decrease in production – the extent of the 'marginal' change – will, of course, be related to the scale of the overall operation. For example, electricity generating companies are most unlikely to be concerned with decisions about whether or not to produce one more watt of electricity!

The concept of the margin is central to most economic decisions and hence is referred to throughout this book, both in terms of consumer behaviour when buying products and the behaviour of firms when deciding whether to alter production. Consumers, through their purchasing decisions, must decide whether or not buying a particular product will add more to their well-being than spending the same amount on some alternative. Similarly, at the heart of managerial decision-making is the question of whether or not the increase in output will provide enough extra revenue to compensate for the extra cost of production. The aim of the manager (i.e. the decision-maker in this case) is to find the optimal level of production.

Business objectives

Traditionally, the study of managerial decision-making has focused on the single objective of profit maximization. This stems from the fact that owners of businesses were considered to be simply interested in making profit. Today, no doubt many businesses are still run with an eye to maximizing profits. However, the development of modern capitalism has led to a divorce of ownership and control in modern companies. Especially in the large companies which dominate production in advanced economies, a 'managerial class' controls the company's operations, while ownership of the company is spread amongst a multitude of shareholders. This development has led to a reassessment of the view that the pursuit of maximum profit is always the firm's primary objective, even in the longer term.

In reality, management in large companies may pursue a wide range of objectives, which may not always be wholly consistent (e.g. maximizing output as against minimizing environmental damage). Profit maximization for shareholders, suitably defined, may be but one element amongst such objectives and may not be of most immediate importance in the eyes of management. Other possible objectives of managers could include the following:

- The achievement of personal goals, involving personal security and reward, status, degree of discretionary power, etc.
- Growth targets for the company in terms of scale of output, market share, geographical market, annual extension of physical capacity, size of departments or size of the labour force, etc.
- Maximization of sales revenue (as opposed to sales volume).

It is possible, of course, that managers at any given time may not be actively attempting to maximize any particular goal, preferring instead to achieve a *satisfactory* level of performance across a range of indicators, including the attainment of simply an adequate level of profits to satisfy shareholders' expectations and thereby retain their confidence (and their own jobs!).

Ascertaining the objective(s) of management is, of course, important as the objective pursued determines actions taken such as, for example, whether to increase or reduce output. Unless we are clear about management's objective(s) it is difficult to say anything useful about the precise decisions which should be taken. It may make sense to increase output to maximize sales revenue but to cut output to maximize profit. Therefore, to aid and simplify the analysis we shall normally assume that managers aim to maximize profit. We choose profit because most firms seem to strive for higher and higher profits and because even where managers pursue other ends they are unlikely to be entirely disinterested in profitability (or at least their shareholders are unlikely to be disinterested!).

In Chapter 5 we return to the discussion of managerial objectives and observe how other objectives alter conclusions about optimal prices and outputs based on the profit-maximizing assumption.

Time dimension

Managerial decisions and objectives need to be considered within a time framework – profit maximization in the short term may not be consistent with the long-term success of the company. In certain circumstances it may even lead to the downfall of the company in the long term. For example, short-term profit maximization might mean that workers are pushed so hard to increase production for relatively low wages that they eventually go on strike, or that goods are made which are less reliable and sold at such high prices that new competitors eventually emerge to take over the market. This suggests that profit maximization (and other managerial objectives) can only usefully be discussed in relation to a given time dimension.

Time is a continuum, but for convenience economists normally distinguish between the following two broad time periods, which are referred to as the *short run* and the *long run*:

- **The short run represents the operating period of the business in which at least one factor of production is fixed in supply**. This means that, for example, as the firm attempts to increase output by employing more and more of one resource alongside a fixed resource, diminishing marginal returns set in. For example, employing more and more workers on an existing assembly line is likely to lead to overcrowding and a reduction in productivity, i.e. output per worker. Ultimately, there will be one level of production in the short run which is the most cost efficient and that can be attained given existing resources. This will be at some point on the firm's production possibility curve (referred to earlier) depending upon the costs of producing the different products.

- **The long run represents the planning horizon for the firm**. This is the period in which all factors of production may be varied, e.g. more workers can be employed or made redundant, land can be acquired or sold off, and capital equipment can be bought or scrapped. In other words, the *scale* of production can be changed over the long-term planning horizon to enable the firm to arrive at its long-run optimal level of production, defined in terms of the least cost allocation of resources.

Externalities

So far we have emphasized objectives (short run and long run) from the viewpoint of the firm only. Of course, it may arise that these objectives are not compatible with the interests of society in general. The annual accounts of firms do not reflect so-called *social costs* or *social benefits* (referred to by economists as *externalities*). For example, the expansion of industrial output may increase the firm's profits but damage the environment through pollution (an external cost). Alternatively, the development of a new reservoir may enhance the quality of life for the public in general by increasing the provision of water sports (an external benefit), while at the same time benefiting the water company.

Managers of firms operating in the private sector are likely to find it difficult to incorporate such externalities into their decision-making either because they may lose out to competitors who are less socially conscious, or because there is no direct return to the shareholders. However, it is becoming increasingly important to managers in today's society to pay greater and greater attention to these issues as public awareness of environmental issues increases – being 'green' increasingly plays a part in a modern business strategy. Business decisions will then reflect both the *internal* costs and benefits of a project to the firm (the costs and benefits they directly control) and those *external* costs and benefits which affect society in general.

Most of the discussion in this book will centre on internal costs and benefits, but this is not intended to imply that private sector managers can safely ignore externalities in the present business environment. Indeed, this is far from being the case. For public sector managers concerned with pursuing social welfare, externalities should be of central concern.

Discounting

In considering all of the costs and benefits of an investment project it is important to appreciate not only externalities but the fact that, because internal and external benefits accrue over the life of the project, they must be *discounted*.

> **The concept of discounting is concerned with the fact that costs and benefits arising in future years are worth less to us than costs and benefits arising today.**

It is natural, for example, to have a preference for money today over money tomorrow. This is not because of uncertainty about future inflation or fears that the money may not arrive tomorrow, but rather it is the property of the passage of time. For example, a rational person faced with a choice between receiving £1,000 now or the same amount in a year's time would choose the former option. This is because the money received now could be invested and earn interest. With an annual interest rate of 10%, the £1,000 would be worth £1,100 in a year's time. The fact that interest can be earned over time means that, even with zero inflation, all future costs and revenues must be discounted at an appropriate rate of interest (discount rate) before we are able to make proper comparisons with costs and revenues expressed in current values.

The importance of discounting is greatest when a decision has to be made between different investment projects over different time periods which therefore produce alternative streams of returns. The proper evaluation of these alternatives requires the use of an appropriate discount rate since an investment decision involves the commitment of resources today in order to achieve an annual stream of outputs in the future. Leaving aside the possibility of liquidating the assets, resources invested are committed for the lifetime of the project. The future values may be discounted to net present values (NPV) by adapting the standard formula for compound interest. For instance, with an interest rate of 10%, a receipt of £1,100 in one year hence is equivalent to the receipt of £1,000 today. The *discounting formula* is expressed generally as:

$$\text{NPV} = \sum \frac{S_t}{(1 + r)^t}$$

where NPV is the present value of the net cash flow over the life of the project, S is the future sum, r is the rate of interest or discount rate, and t the number of years elapsing before the future sum is received. The rate of interest in this formula reflects the opportunity cost of the funds invested over the life, t, of the project (note that the symbol Σ is shorthand notation for 'the sum of' such that the value of $S_t/(1+r)^t$ for each year is summed over all years of the project life).

A simple example should make the discounting principle clearer. Suppose a landowner is due to receive a net annual rent from his property (rent less repairs and other costs) of £5,000 each year over the life of a four-year agreement. It is expected that the rate of interest on bank deposits will remain fixed at 10%. The present value of the future stream of rental income is calculated as follows:

$$\text{NPV} = \frac{£5,000}{(1+0.10)} + \frac{£5,000}{(1+0.10)^2} + \frac{£5,000}{(1+0.10)^3} + \frac{£5,000}{(1+0.10)^4}$$

$$= \frac{£5,000}{1.10} + \frac{£5,000}{1.21} + \frac{£5,000}{1.331} + \frac{£5,000}{1.4641}$$

$$= £4,545.45 + £4,132.23 + £3,756.57 + £3,415.07$$

$$= £15,849.32$$

The landowner should compare this net present value of £15,849.32 with alternative returns that could be earned if the property was used in other ways, with the appropriate net revenue stream, similarly discounted, to check whether or not a rental income of £5,000 per year is adequate (it should be noted that there is usually no need to work through calculations such as those above since computer programs and discount tables are readily available and greatly simplify the computations involved).

The competitive environment

A recurring theme in this book is the question of managerial behaviour in terms of objectives and outcomes. An important factor in determining this behaviour is the nature of the competitive environment in which the firm operates. As all managers are aware, decision-making within the firm is to a large extent influenced, or at least constrained, by the fact that the firm needs to operate successfully in the market place in order to survive. Therefore, the form that the market takes usually influences the forms of action adopted by management and, in turn, ultimately business success or failure. In other words, the existence and the structure of the competitive environment are significant in explaining decisions taken relating to marketing, research and development, production, finance, strategic planning, distribution and so on. In this book we analyze in some detail the structure of the competitive environment, especially in Chapter 4. But briefly at this stage, the competitive environment may be viewed as a spectrum of competition ranging from a perfectly competitive market structure to one which is highly monopolistic. Economists break this spectrum down into four discrete models of market structure, namely:

- Perfectly competitive markets.
- Monopolistically competitive markets.
- Oligopolistic competition.
- Monopoly.

We briefly describe the nature of each of these market structures in turn.

Perfectly competitive markets

These are markets which are made up of numerous small firms each offering identical products with complete freedom of entry for new firms. In such markets each firm has no control over the price of the product – each is a *price-taker* rather than a *price-maker* – and must accept the price determined by the interaction of the overall market supply and demand. Closest examples tend to be found in commodity markets (wheat, coffee, timber, etc.).

Monopolistically competitive markets

These markets arise, as in the perfectly competitive case, where there are very many sellers but where there is also some degree of differentiation of the product offered by each. In such situations, each firm has some degree of monopoly power, in so far as it may be able to influence the price of its product to a degree that is independent of its competitors. Nevertheless, the degree of pricing discretion that each firm has is limited. Closest examples tend to be found in the retailing and services sectors, e.g. grocery sales through the use of branded products and hairdressing where stylists have different reputations.

Oligopolistic competition

This form of market arises where there exists a small number of relatively large firms which are constantly wary of each other's actions regarding price and non-price competition. There is therefore a high degree of interdependence in oligopolistic markets between the competing firms. In principle the products on offer may be undifferentiated, but in practice some differentiation usually exists. This type of market structure is very common in developed economies. Amongst the industries which are most obviously oligopolistic in such economies are the commercial banking sector and the brewing, motor and oil industries.

Monopoly

At the opposite end of the spectrum from the perfectly competitive market is the sole supplier or monopolist. At the extreme the monopolist faces no competition because there are no other producers of the same or similar products. In practice, it is rare to find such a 'pure' monopoly because it is usually possible to find some, albeit imperfect, substitute, e.g. gas instead of electricity. The definition of a monopoly, therefore, is a fairly arbitrary one and it is common, in practice, to regard a monopoly as existing where the market is dominated by one firm producing a product for which there is no *close* substitute. Where substitution is highly imperfect, the firm will have wide discretion regarding either price or output.

Sometimes it may be difficult to define precisely the form and structure of the competitive environment faced by a firm. However, there are three groups of factors which managers might consider when attempting to determine the nature of the markets in which they are currently operating or are planning to operate. These are:

- the number and size distribution of the buyers and sellers in the market;
- the degree of product differentiation that exists, and
- the severity of the barriers to entry and exit that face potential new entrants to the market.

The significance of these groups of factors in relation to the nature of the market structure described above is summarized in Figure 1.4.

Porter's Five Forces Model

The above discussion of market structure is also usefully encapsulated in the Five Forces Model developed by Michael Porter of Harvard University in which industrial profitability is mainly a function of industry structure. This model describes the competitive environment as being determined by the following forces:

1. **The power of buyers** – how much leverage buyers have in determining the price.
2. **The power of input suppliers** – the competition amongst suppliers which determines the price of inputs to the firm (e.g. components).
3. **The threat from potential new entrants into the industry** – i.e. the degree of market contestability.
4. **The threat from substitute products**.
5. **The degree of competition (rivalry) in the industry**.

The interrelationship between these five forces is graphically expressed in Figure 1.5. Porter argues that they ultimately determine the competitive environment faced by a firm. For example, a firm

THE COMPETITIVE ENVIRONMENT				
	Perfect competition	Monopolistic competition	Oligopoly	Monopoly
Number of buyers and sellers	Very high	Very many	Few suppliers	One supplier (in extreme case of 'pure' monopoly)
Degree of product differentiation	Nil	Very low	Usually high	Very high
Market entry and exit barriers	Nil	Nil	High	Very high

MARKET ATTRIBUTES

Figure 1.4 Characteristics of competitive markets

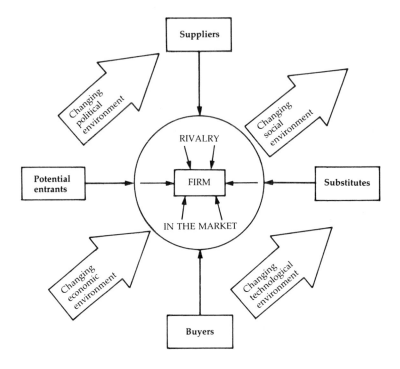

Figure 1.5 Forces shaping the competitive environment

which sells to consumers who have limited buying power, and operates in a market where there is little rivalry, is likely to make more profits than a firm facing the opposite circumstances. The aim of a firm's strategy must therefore be to limit the power of these five forces.

Over time, of course, the competitive environment, as encapsulated in Porter's five forces, will be subject to change – sometimes dramatic change. As illustrated in Figure 1.5, these changes may come in the shape of political, economic, social or technological developments which will often be difficult to predict (managers of former East German factories will certainly support this sentiment!). The challenge facing management, therefore, is a daunting one in that decisions have to be made not only to take account of the competitive dynamics of the market but also in terms of a changing and unpredictable *external environment*.

Awareness of the importance and impact of the external environment on business can be greatly enhanced through the use of PEST analysis (where PEST is shorthand for the 'political, economic, social and technological' factors). The most successful firms are those which do this best. Precisely identifying *which* firms is, however, beyond the scope of the authors of this book! – though we do cling to the belief that where managers are *aware* of the forces impacting on their business, the likelihood of success is vastly improved.

Concluding remarks

The purpose of this chapter has been to provide an overview of the nature of the business environment and its impact on managerial decision-making. We have introduced many of the terms and concepts which form the basis of the discussion in later chapters.

Managers operate in an uncertain world and hence decision-making is not an exact science. It is never possible to predict the future with complete confidence. In particular the behaviour of consumers and the actions and reactions of competitors in the market place will always be uncertain to some degree. Incomplete information dominates in the business world, but through a systematic analysis of problems based on sound economic principles the manager is more likely to be able to minimize the risk of failure and maximize the opportunities presented. Business decision-making is an art, not a science. Nevertheless, the intelligent application of the economic analysis included in this book should help the busy manager to make better choices. In this book we shall be concerned from time to time with economic models in which perfect information is assumed (even though we are all agreed that it does not exist) because by assuming that consumers and producers are perfectly informed, we can predict how purchasing and selling decisions would be affected.

The models, therefore, provide useful insights into the operation of competitive markets. They serve as stepping stones towards a more critical awareness of the pressures and challenges facing management today and allow us to explore the intricacies of business economics within a coherent framework. Once we are clear as to how perfectly informed markets work, with appropriate allowances for information shortcomings, we can better predict how *actual* markets work. We begin our detailed study of the competitive environment by looking at the nature and role of consumer demand.

2

The analysis of consumer demand

The essence of consumer demand

It should not be surprising to discover that successful firms are often those that expend considerable time and effort analyzing the demand for their products. A firm is unlikely to make adequate profits, and hence remain in business for very long, unless it has a reasonable knowledge of the demand conditions facing it in the market place. Complete ignorance of these conditions means that it will have no clear basis – other than guesswork – for deciding how much to produce, what quantity it can expect to sell, and at what price. By contrast, the successful firm plans effectively how to allocate its resources so that it can respond positively to any changes in the demand for its products. For example, it will hold sufficient finished stocks and maintain an adequate stream of work in progress to meet expected surges in demand.

In this chapter we develop a number of economic concepts which are useful to an understanding of consumer behaviour. The key aim is to identify the forces that determine the demand for a firm's product and to show how management can proceed to measure the magnitude and impact of these forces. Therefore, much of what is presented in this chapter provides a foundation for various aspects of business management. For example, if management can estimate the importance of factors such as price, advertising or the rate of interest in determining the quantity demanded, then this will help in planning a useful marketing strategy. At the same time, if it is possible to predict (albeit with some margin of error) the volume of sales that can be expected when one or more of these factors is altered, this will have important implications for the firm's overall financial and business strategies.

Some of the factors affecting the demand for a firm's product are under the direct control of management (such as the advertising spend) while other factors that influence demand are external. External factors include consumers' incomes, the prices charged by competitors, demographic trends and changes in the weather. As they lie outside the firm they may be described as 'uncontrollable' conditions of demand. Business planning should nevertheless incorporate some estimate of how these forces might change in the future and what the ultimate impact of possible changes will be on sales. This leads us into the area of *forecasting* and forecasting methods which we shall return to in Chapter 10. For the moment, however, we shall focus on the measurement and determination of demand, linking the concepts introduced in this chapter to the determination of revenues received from sales and to the overall structure of the industry in question. This provides a useful introduction to the more detailed analysis of market structure and the nature of competition provided in Chapter 4.

Much of what is presented in this chapter represents a simple and practical approach to understanding demand, based on a theoretical foundation developed by various economists over many years. Various models of consumer behaviour have been put forward by economists to provide insights into the decision-making process of consumers. However, they all draw on the (common sense) observation that consumers, when spending their hard-earned money, attempt to increase their *utility* (i.e. overall satisfaction from their limited budgets). In other words, it is (realistically) assumed that all consumers are *rational* in that they desire to maximize their own well-being.

In this chapter the following central concepts are discussed:

- The market demand curve.
- Consumer surplus.
- The determinants of demand.
- The classification of products.
- Concepts of elasticity.
- The relationship between price elasticity and sales revenue.

The market demand curve

When economists discuss the 'demand' for a product, they mean the *effective demand*, that is, the amount consumers are willing to buy at a given price and over a given period of time. Demand, in the economists' sense, does not mean the wants, desires or needs of people since these may not be backed up by the ability to pay (you may *want* a Jaguar motor car but, unless you actually go out and buy one your desire will have no bearing on the demand for Jaguar cars!). Managers refer to demand in the same way, hence readers should have no difficulty with this treatment.

At any given time and for any good or service it is possible to perceive of a consumer's demand curve.

> A *consumer's demand curve* relates the amount the consumer is willing to buy to each conceivable price for the product.

Clearly, we would expect the consumer to be willing to buy more of something the lower its price. From the notion of a relationship between an individual consumer's demand for a product and its price we can derive the total demand of all consumers in the market – the latter in turn gives rise to the notion of an aggregate or *market* demand curve for a product.

> The *market demand curve* is derived by summing the individual demand curves of consumers horizontally.

A market demand curve is shown in Figure 2.1. D_AD_A represents the demand for the product by Adam at various price levels while D_ED_E represents the corresponding demand by Eve. Summing horizontally it will be seen that, for example, at price P_1, a total quantity of $Q_{(A+E)}$ is demanded, which is equal to the sum of the individual quantities demanded, Q_A and Q_E, at that price.

The law of demand

Product demand curves, both individual and market, show the relationship between different possible prices of the good in question and the quantity of the good which we expect to sell.

> In general there is a central *law of demand*, which states that there is an inverse relationship between the price of a good

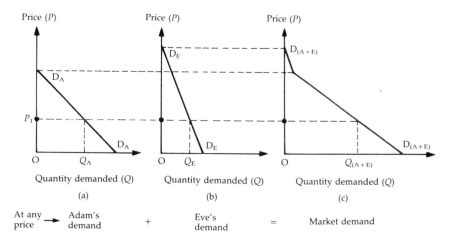

Figure 2.1 Derivation of the market demand curve

and the quantity demanded *assuming all other factors that might influence demand are held constant.*

Thus, if price increases, it is normally the case that less will be bought (and vice versa). In other words, a *rational* consumer prefers to pay less rather than more for something. In this respect we think it is safe to assume that most consumers are rational! Economists are sometimes criticized for assuming 'consumer rationality', but at least in terms of the way in which it is presented here, it does not seem to be an outlandish assumption about consumer behaviour.

It is important to be aware of the significance of the expression 'assuming all other factors that might influence demand are held constant'. Economic activity is complex and usually more than one thing is changing at any given time. For example, at the time a firm is changing the price of a product household incomes may also be increasing, advertising expenditure may be rising, consumers may be revising their attitude to the product and so forth. In order to study the relationship that exists between price and demand, it is necessary to 'freeze' the picture. We can then later study how behaviour changes as we introduce other factors which might impact on demand, step by step. The assumption of 'all other factors held constant' is, therefore, merely a convenient framework to begin the study of what we accept is a much more complex relationship in practice. The assumption is often abbreviated and stated in its Latin form as *ceteris paribus*. Also, by initially examining how demand changes only in relation to changes in price we are able to illustrate the demand relationship in a simple, two-dimensional, diagram.

We stated above that if price increases, demand *normally* falls (and vice versa). The word 'normally' is very important and later we shall examine cases where the law of demand may not apply. For the moment, however, we shall assume that the demand curve is downward sloping from left to right, with price measured on the vertical axis and quantity demanded on the horizontal axis as shown by the line DD in Figure 2.2. Note that if price is continuously increased, a point must eventually be reached where nothing will be demanded, point p' in Figure 2.2. Likewise, management will eventually discover that the only way it can sell more is to give the good away (i.e. charge a zero price – point q' in the figure)! The line DD in Figure 2.2 is referred to, generally, as a demand 'curve', despite the fact that in this diagram it is shown as a straight line. Economists frequently use linear demand curves as approximations for true relationships between price and demand which may in fact be non-linear (such as D'D' in Figure 2.2). This is purely for convenience and illustration in text books, though over small sections of the curve a linear representation will often provide a close enough approximation to predict actual demand in many practical applications.

Consumer surplus

The negative slope of the demand curve illustrated in Figure 2.2 gives rise to a concept that has often been influential in guiding economic policy known as *consumer surplus*. This is defined as follows:

> **A consumer's surplus is the excess of the price which a person would be willing to pay rather than go without the good, over that which he actually does pay**.

This is also sometimes referred to as *consumer's rent*. The magnitude of consumer surplus can be approximated by the area under the demand curve, which represents the additional aggregate payment consumers would pay in excess of the amounts actually paid for a good at the going price. For example, area $p'p''B$ if the product was sold at price p'' in Figure 2.2.

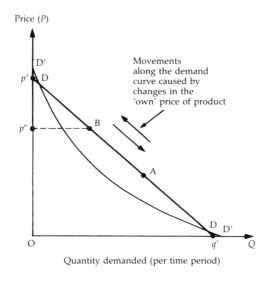

Figure 2.2 Linear and non-linear demand relationships

One way of appreciating the meaning of this concept is to imagine that goods are sold on an open auction basis so that each potential consumer is able to bid the price that he or she is willing to pay – each bid will thus reflect the valuation placed on the good by each individual. If the good is being sold by a discriminating monopolist, the objective would be to ensure that no consumer surplus remains. In other words, everyone will have paid a price that just equals the valuation they have each placed on the good. Consider the value (i.e. price) you would place on a drink of water if you had been in the desert for a week relative to that which someone else in a more 'comfortable' situation would place on it!

The determinants of demand

As we have stated above, the study of consumer behaviour generally shows that as the price of a product falls, consumers will choose to buy more of it, *ceteris paribus*. However, a change in the price of the good itself is only one determinant of the total quantity of the good demanded. A listing of the most important factors which affect demand might include the following:

- The 'own price' of the good itself (P_o).
- The price of substitute goods (P_s).
- The price of complementary goods (P_c).
- The level of advertising expenditure on the product in question, as well as on complementary and substitute products (A).
- The level and distribution of consumers' disposable incomes (Y_d), i.e. income after state direct taxes and benefits.
- Changes in consumers' tastes and preferences (T).
- The cost and availability of credit (C).
- Consumers' expectations concerning future price rises and availability of the product (E).
- Changes in population, if we are examining the total market demand (POP).

In relation to particular products some of these factors may be more important as determinants of demand than others. The factors other than 'own price' which affect demand may generally be described as representing the *conditions of demand* (i.e. the 'environment' within which consumers decide how much to purchase at any given price). We can summarize these conditions in a *demand function*, which in shorthand notation expresses the quantity demanded of a product (Q_d) over a given time period, as:

$$Q_d = f(P_o, P_s, P_c, A, Y_d, T, C, E, \text{POP})$$

Thus, the demand curve (either DD or D'D') in Figure 2.2 shows the quantities of the good in question that will be bought (Q_d) at different prices (P_o) with all the other factors in the demand function held constant. Clearly, as P_o changes, there will be a *movement along* the demand curve, say from A to B (in the case of a price rise) or B to A (in the case of price fall). However, if any of the other factors in the demand function should change, then there will be a *shift* in the demand curve as illustrated in Figure 2.3. This highlights the fact that, as the conditions of demand change (except for P_o, the 'own price'), there will be a new price–quantity relationship established. For example, a population boom is likely to mean that at any given

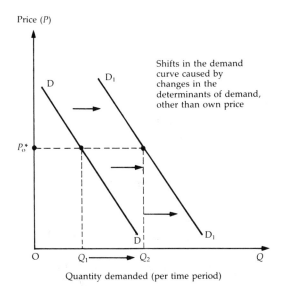

Price (*P*)

Shifts in the demand
curve caused by
changes in the
determinants of demand,
other than own price

Figure 2.3   Shifts in the demand curve

price, P_0^*, more will be demanded over time, shown by the increase
from Q_1 to Q_2 in Figure 2.3.

The distinction between a *movement along* a product's demand
curve and a *shift* in the curve is useful because it helps to identify the
causes and nature of changes in demand.

> **When the own price changes, the outcome is a *movement
> along the demand curve* and when any other determinant of
> demand changes, there will be a *shift of the demand curve*
> (either to the left, showing a fall in the quantity demanded, or
> to the right, showing a rise, depending on the nature of the
> change).**

Some examples of shifts in demand curves are presented in Figure
2.4.

The classification of products

There are two distinct reasons why more of a good is usually
demanded as its price falls (and vice versa). These are referred to as
the 'income effect' and the 'substitution effect' as follows:

- **The income effect**. As its own price falls, consumers are in effect better off and hence able to buy more of the good. The fall in price has raised their effective purchasing power, while the opposite applies in the case of a price rise. The change in price is equivalent, in effect, to a change in income (though *actual* income is unchanged).

- **The substitution effect**. As the price of a product falls, it becomes relatively cheaper than alternatives. Hence, there is a natural tendency for consumers to switch towards the product in question, substituting more of it for other goods. The opposite outcome occurs, of course, where there is a rise in the price of the product.

The substitution effect on demand of a price change will always be opposite in direction to the price change (assuming rational behaviour on the part of consumers) or zero if no substitutes exist at all. The income effect, however, can either increase or reduce demand depending not only on the direction of the income change but on the nature of the good or service. The direction of the income effect allows us to classify the nature of products under the following particular headings:

- **Normal products**. Goods and services may be classified as 'normal products' if the quantity demanded rises as incomes rise and falls as incomes fall. Here, as throughout the rest of the chapter, income refers to a change in real purchasing power rather than simply a nominal change which may be neutralized by a proportionate price change. For example, family cars would be classified as 'normal' since as household incomes rise (in real terms), the demand for such cars also generally rises. Note that the key factor is the link between demand and income – we would still expect an inverse relationship between price and quantity demanded.

- **Inferior products**. Certain products are classified as 'inferior' because the demand for them *falls* as incomes *rise* (and vice versa). For example, as household incomes rise, there may be a tendency to switch from buying cheaper, lower quality meats to buying Grade A beef. The switch from inferior to superior products is common as real incomes rise over time. For most inferior goods, however, there is still likely to be an overall increase in demand as their price falls. This is because the positive substitution effect (i.e. a switch towards the relatively

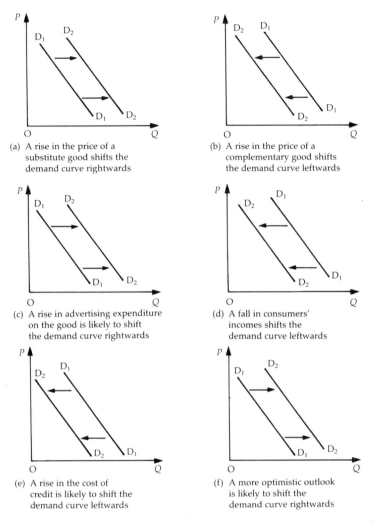

Figure 2.4   Changes in the conditions of demand (demand curves DD refer to good in question)

inexpensive product) more than offsets the negative income effect on demand.

- **Giffen products**. A special case of the inferior product arises when, as price *rises*, more of the good in question is bought – resulting in an *upward* sloping demand curve, contrary to the normal law of demand. Such products are classified as Giffen products, named after a nineteenth-century English economist who studied the response to changes in the price of potatoes in Ireland. Giffen found that as the price of potatoes rose, the Irish at that time bought more since they could not afford to buy as much of the more expensive foodstuffs such as meat. This response to a price change is still found today in many developing countries – as the price of rice rises, people are forced to buy less meat and fish in order to be able to continue buying sufficient quantities of rice to stay alive – hence the vicious circle of famine and malnutrition so common in many parts of Africa. In the case of Giffen products, the income effect of a price change is so large that it swamps the substitution effect, leading to an overall rise (fall) in demand for the product as its price rises (declines).

- **Veblen products**. It has also been suggested that 'luxury type' products also display perverse price–demand relationships, though for different reasons to that of the Giffen products case. These are sometimes referred to as Veblen products, after the American economist, Thorstein Veblen (1857–1929), who explored the phenomenon. For example, as the price of a piece of jewellery rises, the demand for it may also rise as consumers attach a 'snob' value to owning and displaying expensive items. Equally, as the price falls there is the possibility that the product could lose its up-market image – 'everyone can afford it, so why bother to buy it'! This situation reflects a change in tastes, determined by the perception of the product in relation to its price. The existence of a positive Veblen effect is, of course, very advantageous to the producers concerned since it enables them to charge premium prices for their products.

Concepts of elasticity

The discussion so far has been concerned with the broad direction of relationships between price changes, changes in other possible determinants of demand and the quantity demanded. However, in addition to understanding the *nature* of demand, it would of course be very useful if management were able to estimate the *extent* to which demand is likely to respond to a price change. Gauging this responsiveness is referred to by economists as *the measurement of price elasticity*. In addition, since, as we have seen, demand is affected by many factors, we can calculate elasticity (i.e. responsiveness of quantity demanded) with respect to a wide range of variables other than price, notably the price of other goods and income. Thus we can define the following

- **Price elasticity of demand**. This measures the responsiveness of quantity demanded of a product to changes in its 'own price'. For example, if the price of alcohol increases, what happens to the quantity of alcohol demanded?
- **Cross-price elasticity of demand**. This measures the responsiveness of quantity demanded to changes in the prices of other goods (both complements and substitutes). For example, if the price of one brand of coffee rises, what happens to the demand for another coffee brand? Or, if the price of petrol falls, what happens to the demand for cars?
- **Income elasticity of demand**. This measures the responsiveness of demand to a change in the real income of consumers. For example, if real incomes are rising, on average, by £100 per month, what will happen to the demand for housing?

In general terms, a *coefficient of elasticity* can be calculated for each of the above categories using the following general formula:

$$\text{Coefficient of elasticity} = \frac{\text{Percentage change in quantity demanded}}{\text{Percentage change in the relevant variable}}$$

We will now examine each of these three elasticity concepts in more detail.

Price elasticity of demand

Based on the general formula, the (own) price elasticity of demand for a product may be defined as:

$$E_d = \frac{\text{Percentage change in quantity demanded}}{\text{Percentage change in the price of the product}}$$

Where a product has a downward sloping demand curve (the usual case), the value of the price elasticity of demand will always be negative – since when price rises demand falls and when price falls demand rises. Conventionally, however, the negative sign is omitted when the value of elasticity is stated and we follow this convention in the following discussion.

Two different types of price elasticity (E_d) can be calculated as follows:

- **arc** elasticity of demand, and
- **point** elasticity of demand.

Arc elasticity of demand

With reference to Figure 2.5, arc elasticity measures the responsiveness of demand between two points on the demand curve such as X and Y, whereas, as the name suggests, point elasticity is concerned with the elasticity at only one given point of the curve. Since managers are usually concerned with estimating the effect on demand of, say, a 5% rise in price, the price change causes a movement along a section of the demand curve and hence the arc elasticity formula is the one that is often used for practical purposes.

Using the notation shown in Figure 2.5, we can calculate arc elasticity as:

$$
\text{Arc } E_d = \frac{(Q_2 - Q_1)/\tfrac{1}{2}(Q_2 + Q_1)}{(P_2 - P_1)/\tfrac{1}{2}(P_2 + P_1)}
$$

$$
= \frac{(Q_2 - Q_1)}{(P_2 - P_1)} \times \frac{(P_2 + P_1)}{(Q_2 + Q_1)}
$$

It is important to appreciate the reason why arc elasticity is expressed on the basis of the average quantity, $\tfrac{1}{2}(Q_2 + Q_1)$, and average price, $\tfrac{1}{2}(P_2 + P_1)$. When there is an appreciable price change, the value of elasticity calculated on the basis of X as the starting point will differ from that calculated on the basis of Y as the starting point – we end up with two· different values for the sensitivity of demand to price changes which will not be very useful in business decisions. Using the midpoint, however, ensures that price elasticity is the same regardless of the direction of movement on the demand curve and, since it is based on the average price and

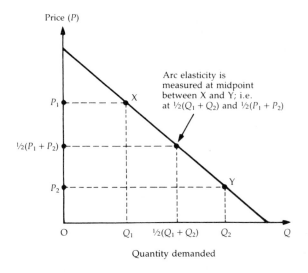

Figure 2.5 Arc elasticity of demand

average quantity, it will be closer to the true estimate of elasticity over the price range than that based on either of the two extreme points.

Point elasticity of demand

It should be intuitively clear from Figure 2.5 that as X and Y come closer together, the arc shrinks in size and the two values for elasticities calculated at X and Y separately will get closer to each other. If the distance is negligible, the arc will end up as a single point and the arc elasticity calculation can be replaced by that for *point elasticity*.

Point elasticity is defined as:

$$\text{Point } E_d = \frac{(Q_2 - Q_1)/Q_1}{(P_2 - P_1)/P_1}$$

$$= \frac{(Q_2 - Q_1)}{(P_2 - P_1)} \times \frac{P_1}{Q_1}$$

While point elasticity is expressed here in relation to Q_1 and P_1 it will be appreciated that since the difference between Q_1 and Q_2 and P_1

and P_2 will be infinitesimally small, it no longer matters whether we use the initial or final price and quantity values. In business, of course, management is unlikely to be interested in 'infinitesimally' small changes in price since it is impractical to introduce, say, a 0.0001% change in the retail price of most products! However, while arc elasticity seems to be the more useful estimator for managers wrestling with the likely effects on the demand for their product of a price change, point elasticity has a role in demand forecasting based on the mathematical techniques introduced in Chapter 10.

The terms 'elastic' and 'inelastic' are often used to describe different degrees of elasticity. In general (and ignoring the negative sign):

- Products with a price elasticity of demand of less than 1 are said to have a relatively inelastic demand with respect to price – they are said to be **price inelastic**.

- Products with a price elasticity of demand greater than 1 are said to have a relatively elastic demand – they are said to be **price elastic**.

- Products with a price elasticity of demand equal to 1 are said to have a **unit elasticity** of demand.

Irrespective of the precise method of calculation, the value of the resulting price elasticity of demand will vary depending upon the nature of the demand for the good in question. In Figure 2.6 the following three extreme price elasticities are illustrated (a, b and c) together with a representation (d) of the elasticities along a downward sloping demand curve:

- **Perfectly inelastic demand**. When the demand for a product is entirely unresponsive to any change in price, the demand curve will be a vertical line as shown in Figure 2.6(a) with E_d equal to zero at every point. This is referred to as a perfectly inelastic demand.

- **Perfectly elastic demand**. Where the demand curve is horizontal, any quantity of the product can be sold at a certain price, P_1, as in Figure 2.6(b). Demand is said to be perfectly elastic with a value of infinity at this price. Any increase in the price, no matter how small, will result in none of the product being sold. If the price is reduced, even marginally, demand (theoretically) becomes infinite.

- **Unit elasticity of demand**. A further special case arises when the

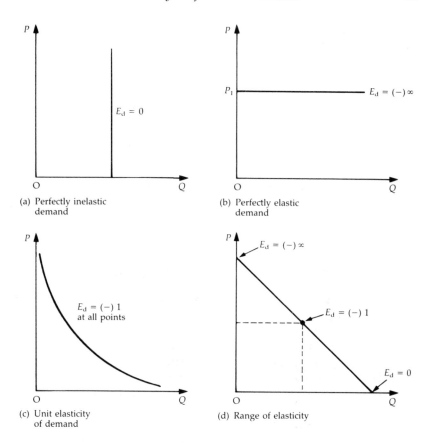

Figure 2.6 Degrees of elasticity of demand

shape of the demand curve is a rectangular hyperbola as in Figure 2.6(c). At any point on it the value of elasticity is equal to unity.

The three cases above are, in practice, rarely found and should be treated as theoretical benchmarks for an analysis of actual price elasticities. Small stretches of a demand curve though may closely equate to one or other of these extremes. Figure 2.6(d) shows a situation where the value of elasticity varies between zero and infinity along its length with a value of 1 at the midpoint. It is important to appreciate that (excluding the cases of vertical and horizontal demand curves) even where a product has a linear demand curve, its elasticity changes as price is altered. This follows because the original price and quantity figures, which enter into the elasticity calculation (see above), change. This means that price elasticity *must* be recalculated for every price change. If the price elasticity was, say, 0.6 when the price was last increased by 5%, even if in the meantime none of the conditions of demand have altered – i.e. the demand curve has not shifted (which in itself is most unlikely) – a further 5% increase in price is likely to be associated with a price elasticity above 0.6.

Given that the price elasticity of demand is a numerical measure of the responsiveness of quantity demanded to changes in price, there is obviously a relationship between the value of the elasticity and the total sales revenue received by the firm. This has important implications for pricing strategy and we shall return to it later in this chapter. First, we introduce the other elasticity of demand measures noted earlier, namely *cross-price* and *income elasticity*.

Cross-price elasticity of demand

Cross-price elasticity of demand (sometimes simply referred to as 'cross-elasticity') indicates the responsiveness of the demand for one product to changes in the prices of other goods or services. The concept has most relevance where there are obvious substitute or complementary commodities and it is, therefore, of key importance to businesses which face major competition or whose sales vary directly with the sales of other goods, e.g. mortgages and mortgage protection insurance.

If A is the good or service we are interested in and B is the other product whose price is altering, we can calculate the value of the cross-price elasticity of demand for A with respect to B as:

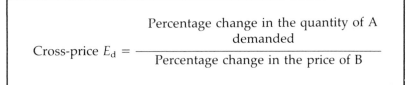

$$\text{Cross-price } E_d = \frac{\text{Percentage change in the quantity of A demanded}}{\text{Percentage change in the price of B}}$$

In the case of substitutes, the resulting figure will be *positive* since a fall in the price of a substitute will lead to more sales of the substitute and hence a fall in the demand for the other product being considered. In the case of complementary products, the resultant value will be *negative*. If the demands for the two goods appear to be unrelated then, of course, the cross-price elasticities between them can be expected to be negligible or zero.

The terminology regarding the degree of cross-price elasticity (ignoring the sign) is the same as for price elasticity, namely:

- 1 = unit cross-price elasticity.
- Less than 1 = inelastic cross-price elasticity.
- Greater than 1 = elastic cross-price elasticity.

Income elasticity of demand

As noted earlier, demand is also likely to be responsiveness to factors other than 'own price' or the price of complements and substitutes. One important factor is real income (i.e. nominal income adjusted for inflation). Empirical studies usually define nominal income in terms of either household disposable income (i.e. household income after income tax, and other direct taxes, plus welfare state payments have been incorporated) or gross national income. Income elasticity of demand is defined as:

$$\text{Income } E_d = \frac{\text{Percentage change in quantity demanded}}{\text{Percentage change in real income}}$$

The value of the income elasticity will usually be positive, suggesting that more is bought as real income rises, though for certain products it may be negative as we saw earlier, albeit in a slightly different context. The actual values of income elasticities can be used to classify products into the following two broad categories:

- **Inferior goods.** These are goods of which consumers buy less when real incomes rise. The value of income elasticity is, therefore, negative. Examples might be potatoes, Lada cars, cheap package holidays, etc.

- **Normal goods.** These are the most common goods with demand generally rising as real income rises. They can themselves be further subdivided into two categories:

  (a) *Necessities.* These are goods and services which exhibit a positive income elasticity of demand, though the value will tend to be less than 1. Articles such as basic foodstuffs and ordinary day-to-day clothing fall into this category. Consumers will purchase a certain amount of these goods at very low levels of income, but they will tend for any given percentage increase in real income to increase their spending on the goods by a smaller proportion.

(b)   *Luxuries.* At very low income levels, nothing will be spent on these but, once a certain threshold level is reached, the proportionate rise in demand for luxury goods is greater than the proportionate rise in real income, e.g. foreign holidays, eating out and video recorders.

From the above classification it is obvious that it will pay firms which want to expand output to concentrate on selling products with high income elasticities when living standards are rising. With greater purchasing power, people will tend to buy disproportionately more luxury-type goods. On the other hand, firms producing goods with low income elasticities will tend to face a more stable market for their products and will be less affected in times of economic downturn. The food retailing industry is usually an example of this.

The relationship between price elasticity and sales revenue

In addition to income elasticity, a firm's fortunes will also be affected by price elasticity as demand, and hence the firm's revenue, changes as a result of price changes. The total receipts or total revenue (TR) earned by a business from sales is calculated by multiplying the total output sold (Q) by the average unit price (P), i.e. $TR = P \times Q$. The resulting value of total revenue is illustrated by the shaded area in Figure 2.7 with price at P_1 and quantity demanded equal to Q_1. Where there is unit elasticity of demand, as the price is varied the total revenue earned from sales remains unchanged. For example, a 1% fall in price will bring about a 1% rise in sales, leaving total revenue unaltered. However, as we indicated earlier, unit elasticity is an extreme case and unlikely to be found over more than modest stretches of a demand curve. It will usually be the case that the value of elasticity will vary along the demand curve, as shown earlier in Figure 2.6(d). As price changes by a certain proportion, the quantity demanded usually changes by a greater or lesser proportion.

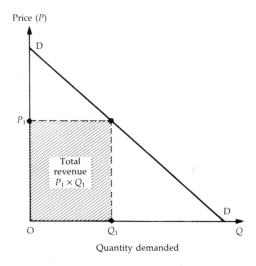

Figure 2.7 Demand and total revenue

In general, we can derive the following rules:

- With a price inelastic demand:
  (a) an increase in price causes a reduction in quantity demanded, but total revenue increases;
  (b) a fall in price causes an increase in quantity demanded, but total revenue earned declines.
- With a price elastic demand:
  (a) an increase in price causes such a large fall in sales that total revenue falls;
  (b) a reduction in price causes such a large increase in the quantity demanded that the total revenue rises.

Hence, it is clear that accurate estimates of price elasticity are vital to business decision-making. Putting this another way, ignorance of the market response to price changes is likely to be a recipe for disaster!

The link between total revenue and price elasticity results from the fact that, faced with a downward sloping demand curve for a product, management must lower price if they want to sell more (other factors held constant). But if extra sales compensate for the lower unit price then total revenue will not decline. Similarly, management might raise the price of a product to raise revenues, but the resulting collapse of demand may actually cause total revenue to contract. In other words, the precise *responsiveness* of demand to a price change determines the effect of a price change on revenue received. This introduces another important concept which will be used throughout much of the remainder of this book, namely *marginal revenue*.

Marginal revenue

Marginal revenue is defined as the change in total revenue as a firm sells one more or one less unit of its output.

The size of a 'unit' will vary from firm to firm – for example, the smallest unit of water which is charged to domestic users is likely to be much more than a single litre, while the car dealer may be concerned with the sale of a single car. To be mathematically correct, marginal revenue is the increase in total revenue resulting from an infinitesimally small change in quantity sold. But it can be approximated by looking at the change in total revenue resulting from a small, quantifiable, change in output.

Figure 2.8 shows the relationship between elasticity, total revenue, marginal revenue (MR) and the demand curve (D). The demand curve is also the average revenue (AR) curve because it shows the price at which each unit is sold. Provided that when units are sold they are all sold at the same price, price and average revenue must be identical.

The key points to note are as follows:

- **The marginal revenue curve declines at twice the rate of the demand (average revenue) curve**. Hence, the marginal revenue curve cuts the horizontal axis at a point mid-way between the origin and point C in the Figure 2.8. A proof of this mathematical relationship is given at the end of the chapter.

- **When total revenue is increasing, marginal revenue is positive**. This results from the fact that demand is elastic between points A and B on the demand curve DD in Figure 2.8.

- **When total revenue is falling, marginal revenue is negative**. A negative marginal revenue value means that demand is inelastic between points B and C in Figure 2.8.

- **Total revenue is maximized when marginal revenue is zero which occurs when the price elasticity is unitary**. Therefore, further attempts to increase total revenue by lowering price

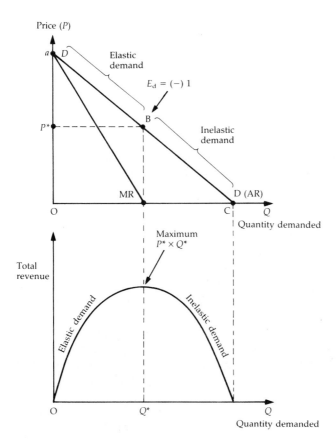

Figure 2.8 Elasticity, marginal revenue and total revenue

below P^* will fail since sales volume will not increase sufficiently to compensate for the price fall.

Marginal revenue is concerned with changes in total revenue resulting from small changes in sales. Since many business decisions hang on whether to increase or reduce sales, the concept of marginal revenue is central to much of the discussion relating to business decision-making in subsequent chapters. It is important, therefore, that the reader should not proceed further until the concept is fully understood.

Concluding remarks

This chapter has been concerned with consumer demand and, specifically, with shedding light on the relationship between the price of a product and the quantity demanded. As we have seen, normally when the price of a product is reduced the quantity demanded by consumers rises. The precise relationship between demand and price depends upon the shape of the product's demand curve and can be measured using the concept of *price elasticity*. But for some goods and services demand may be as much, or more, affected by changes in the *conditions of demand*, notably the price of substitutes or complementary products and changes in consumers' incomes. This chapter has also, therefore, been concerned with exploring the relationship between demand and certain non-price factors. The relationship between price and revenues and the importance of non-price factors in the 'marketing mix' is probed further in Chapter 6.

Of course, the practising manager might object that he or she has insufficient information to construct relevant demand curves. Often the manager may possess, at best, only an intuitive feel for the effect of a price increase or reduction. The demand relationship is also likely to be clouded by uncertainty as to how rival producers might react to a price change – an issue pursued at length in Chapter 4. Economists recognize that business decisions usually have to be made in the face of incomplete, and often very fragmentary, information. The analysis in this chapter has been designed simply to provide a framework for decision-making. It is not intended to imply that economists believe that managers can (or should) estimate their full demand curves. But it is important that managers appreciate that their products *do* have demand curves, even if they find it difficult or impossible to construct them accurately. When the price of a firm's product changes or there are changes in other factors, such as consumers' incomes, demand is very likely to be affected. An ability to separate out the different influences on the demand for a product and an awareness of the likely elasticities are important assets for any manager planning his or her business strategy, as is a knowledge of the nature of the relevant costs of production, to which we now turn.

Note: Proof that the marginal revenue curve declines at twice the rate of the demand curve:

Equation of linear demand relationship:

$$P = a - bQ$$

$$
\begin{aligned}
\text{Total revenue (TR)} &= P \times Q \\
&= (a - bQ) \times Q \\
&= aQ - bQ^2
\end{aligned}
$$

Marginal revenue (MR) is defined as the change in total revenue with respect to a unit change in sales. In terms of differential calculus:

$$
\begin{aligned}
\text{MR} &= \frac{d\text{TR}}{dQ} \\
&= \frac{d(aQ - bQ^2)}{dQ} \\
&= a - 2bQ
\end{aligned}
$$

Thus, comparing the equation for marginal revenue with that for the demand curve we see that both have the same intercept on the vertical axis (equal to a in Figure 2.8) but that the marginal revenue curve has a slope that (in absolute terms) is twice that of the demand curve (i.e. $2b$ compared with b).

3

The analysis of production costs

The essence of production costs

In the previous chapter we discussed the behaviour of consumers and how they react to changes in prices and other variables determining the demand for goods and services. In this chapter we examine the internal operations of business by analyzing the nature of costs of production and the impact costs have on business decision-making. Some of the questions which managers face are as follows:

- Whether to increase or reduce production at the margin as bottlenecks are reached?
- Whether to increase production using more labour?
- Whether or not to increase the overall scale of production by expanding to a new plant size?

Just as consumers, given limited incomes, make decisions about what goods to buy and in what quantity, so managers must make decisions about *how much* to produce (the size of output) and *how* to produce, in terms of the combination of inputs (i.e. labour, raw materials, capital equipment and so on), again with limited resources. These decisions will depend heavily on the relevant costs of production. In this chapter, the following concepts are covered:

- The production function.
- Variable costs versus fixed costs.
- Production decisions in the short run and long run.
- Diminishing returns in production.
- Maximizing profit and the production decision.
- Economies and diseconomies of scale.
- The experience curve.
- Optimal scale and x-inefficiency.
- The firm's supply curve.
- Elasticity of supply.

In managerial decision-making, an understanding of the firm's costs of production and how they change as output is increased or reduced is essential. Of course, behind increases and reductions in costs of production lie considerable changes in the internal workings of the firm. Hence the good manager constantly keeps in mind the impact of output decisions on the so-called 'stakeholders' in the firm: employees, shareholders, suppliers, customers, etc. Other management subjects such as corporate strategy and organizational behaviour deal with the internal decision-making process within firms and the effect this has on outcomes. In contrast, economists are more concerned with the nature of the relationship between the firm and its market – the *competitive environment* – and more specifically the relationship between output, price and costs of production, which in turn affects the employment of factors of production. We therefore start this chapter by considering the relationship between inputs and outputs as described by the *production function*.

The production function

Firms are essentially involved in adding value by converting inputs into outputs. Firms employ labour, purchase materials and components, and invest in land, buildings, plant and equipment with a view to maximizing the amount of output that can be derived from these inputs. These inputs can be combined in different ways (e.g. labour intensive versus capital intensive production) and we might expect the decision as to the precise combination used to be related directly to the costs of different forms of production. In this discussion we adopt the position that managers are interested in minimizing the cost of producing any given output, though we acknowledge that in practice there may be constraints (e.g. union manning agreements) which prevent the kind of smooth adjustment process as set out in the following discussion. Throughout most of the discussion in this chapter it is assumed that the firm is not wasting resources, that is to say, it is assumed that it is minimizing its costs of production at any given output. We directly address the issue of 'inefficiency' towards the end of the chapter.

The production function is a mathematical expression which relates the quantity of all inputs to the quantity of outputs assuming that managers employ all inputs efficiently.

In general terms the production function for any firm may be expressed as follows:

$$Q = F(I_1, I_2, I_3 \ldots I_n)$$

This expression is a shorthand notation to show that the quantity (Q) of output produced is determined by (or a function (F) of) a range of inputs (I_1 to I_n). The inputs or factors of production I_1 to I_n are classified by economists under the general headings of labour, land and capital though the production function can equally relate output to different *types* of labour, capital, etc.

It may not always be obvious to managers what the precise technical relationship is between their firms' inputs and outputs. However, it must be the case that there is a relationship and economists have derived a number of general mathematical forms to describe typical relationships. (A discussion of these relationships is, however, beyond the scope of this book but those interested in delving deeper into this subject should read, e.g. D. F. Heathfield and S. Wise, *An Introduction to Cost and Production Functions*, Macmillan, 1987.)

Variable costs versus fixed costs

In the production process some costs are fixed in the sense that they do not vary as output changes. For example, the lease rent on an office and the capital cost of a computer (including interest charges) are examples of costs which once incurred usually remain the same as output rises – the *fixed factors of production*. In contrast, those costs which do change with output are known as the variable costs. If more goods or services are produced, more inputs are employed and variable costs increase. The kind of inputs involved are raw materials, components, energy, telephone usage and, often, staffing levels – the *variable factors of production*.

It is useful to analyze the way in which fixed costs and variable costs behave as the level of production changes. Such analysis allows us to identify whether or not resources are being used most efficiently. If total fixed costs and total variable costs are averaged over the various levels of output, we can derive values for *average fixed costs* (AFC) and *average variable costs* (AVC). Combining the AFC and the AVC gives *average total costs* (ATC). These costs are illustrated in Figure 3.1. The key points to note about the nature of these costs are the following:

- **Average fixed costs.** As the fixed costs are distributed across more and more output, the average fixed costs decline continuously until at very large output levels they are negligible.

- **Average variable costs.** Average variable costs may fall initially but after a certain level of output they begin to rise. This occurs because of what economists term the *law of diminishing returns*, mentioned in Chapter 1 and discussed more fully below. It is, of course, possible for average variable costs to rise continuously as output expands (as in Figure 3.1), while in some businesses there may be a large output range over which they are constant.

- **Average total costs.** Average total costs, being the combination of AFC and AVC, tend to decline initially and then rise after a certain level of output is reached. Average total cost is often referred to by accountants as the *unit cost*. It is also often referred to as *average cost*.

The extent to which a firm can alter its factors of production is dependent upon the time period concerned. In general, the longer

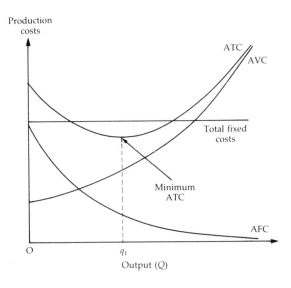

Figure 3.1   The costs of production

the time period the more scope a firm has to vary its inputs. The importance of the *time dimension* in production decisions gives rise to the concepts of the *short run* and *long run*, which we introduced earlier (Chapter 1).

Production decisions in the short run and long run

In Chapter 1 we observed that economists single out two general time periods: the short run and the long run. It is worth repeating the definitions here as follows:

● The **short run** is the time period during which the amount of at least one input is fixed in supply (e.g. the amount of capital equipment installed or in some organizations the number of personnel employed) but the other inputs can be altered. In essence, the short run is the *operating period* of the firm where the management has already made a technical decision about the production process: for example, in a bank so many cashiers are employed using a given number of automatic teller machines in a particular branch. To expand the volume (output) of service it may be possible to employ more staff relatively quickly, but to expand the floor area of the branch and to incorporate more capital equipment will usually take much more time and planning.

- The **long run**, therefore, represents a sufficient length of time for management to be able to vary *all* inputs into the production process. This is also known as the *planning horizon* of the firm in contrast to the current operating period. For example, in order to meet a growing demand from customers the bank's management may decide over the next five years to purchase a much larger building capable of housing many more cash machines and employing a much larger number of staff. The bank will therefore over this period have moved from one *scale* of operation to another which in turn will give rise to a different set of cost relationships.

It is important to appreciate that the terms short run and long run should not be interpreted too rigidly. They are defined according to the extent to which the firm is able to alter its inputs and this will vary from business to business. For example, in large-scale manufacturing plants with high set-up costs, it is obviously difficult to expand production quickly beyond the capacity of the plant, though it may be possible to achieve this over a longer time period through more investment. The length of time in the case of nuclear power generation is many years, while, by contrast, in service-orientated businesses the planning period may be relatively short. In parts of the service sector a shortage of skilled labour may be the major constraint on the expansion of output in the short run. It may be quicker to buy and install a new microcomputer than to train new staff.

Diminishing returns in production

Assuming that the firm is using its existing resources efficiently, the extent to which output can be increased is dependent upon the extent to which inputs can be varied. In the short run, as more and more variable inputs are applied to the fixed factors of production, we tend to find that at first average (unit) costs fall but eventually they begin to rise because diminishing returns set in. Economists refer to this trend as *the law of diminishing returns,* a concept introduced in Chapter 1 but developed here. It is easy to think of cases where this will occur in manufacturing. For example, if the Ford motor company faces a sudden surge in demand for its Escort range of cars and attempts to meet this extra demand by simply employing more workers on a given assembly line, a point will be reached when manning exceeds the optimal level and unit costs rise. Therefore, if the company believes that the increase in demand is permanent, it would be better to begin planning an increase in capacity. Diminishing returns also apply in the service sector. For instance, imagine a retail store attempting to serve more and more customers by simply employing additional sales assistants but without extra cash registers – long queues would be a reflection of diminishing returns in this case.

The output at which average costs are at their lowest is known as the *technically optimum output,* and is output q_1, in Figure 3.1. At this point the factors of production are being combined so as to minimize unit costs. To pursue this discussion of costs further, we now return to the concept of *the margin,* again introduced in Chapter 1.

The change in total costs of production as output is changed is referred to as *the marginal cost.* Marginal cost is correctly defined as the additional cost incurred of producing *one more unit of output,* though in practice it is often applied in general terms to any appropriate increment in production, e.g. the addition to total electricity generating costs of bringing into service the marginal power station. In such cases, however, it is more correct to describe the change in cost as the *incremental cost* rather than marginal cost, incremental cost being the change in total costs associated with a specified change in output, which is not necessarily a single unit. By so doing, we are able to distinguish the incremental cost from the marginal cost.

Marginal costs in the short run will only depend on changes in variable costs because fixed costs are unaltered. In the long run marginal costs reflect changes in the total costs of production since all inputs are variable. Hence, when discussing changes in output we need to distinguish the impact on marginal costs in the short run and long run. Figure 3.2 illustrates a typical relationship between short-run marginal cost and output (the nature of the long-run marginal cost is addressed later in a discussion of economies and diseconomies of scale).

At the margin, as output is increased the additional costs of

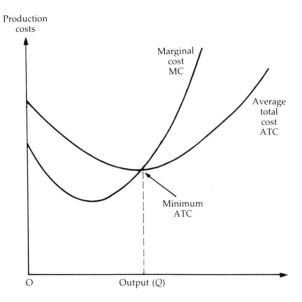

Figure 3.2 Marginal cost and output

production will tend to fall at first but rise as diminishing returns set in, as illustrated in Figure 3.2. There is an important relationship between marginal and average total costs as shown in this figure. As long as the marginal cost (MC) is less than the average total cost (ATC) of production, then the latter must be falling. Once marginal cost exceeds average total cost the latter will be rising. If you have difficulty understanding this relationship, think about the effect on the average score of a sports team when the last player scores more or less than the average scored by the previous players.

In Figure 3.2 above, the marginal cost curve fell and then rose. However, empirical studies of firms suggest that sometimes marginal costs do not vary greatly with the level of output but instead are broadly constant over a certain range of output.

The flatness of the marginal cost curve between outputs of q_1 and q_2 in Figure 3.3 means that average variable costs remain constant until around capacity output is reached. Only variable costs have a bearing on marginal costs because fixed costs are fixed. Often, of course, marginal costs will start to rise before absolute full capacity working is reached as management tries to squeeze out further output.

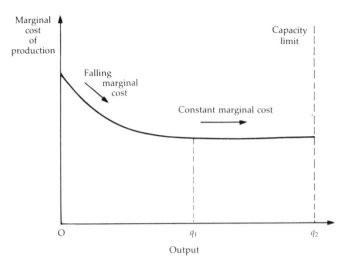

Figure 3.3 Constant marginal costs

Maximizing profit and the production decision

The general rule regarding whether to expand production relates marginal costs to sales revenue. Where a firm is attempting to maximize its profits, as long as the marginal cost of producing one more unit of output is less than the addition to revenue resulting from producing and selling that unit, then it will pay the firm to continue expanding production (additional revenue exceeds additional costs). This is illustrated in Figure 3.4 where MR is the marginal revenue (the addition to total revenue) from selling one more unit. From the discussion in Chapter 2, most firms face a downward sloping demand curve for their product, hence increasing sales is associated (*ceteris paribus*) with a lower price. It follows, therefore, as we saw in that chapter, that the marginal revenue curve will also be downward sloping. To the right of output q^* marginal cost exceeds marginal revenue, therefore the marginal output beyond q^* costs more to produce than the extra revenue generated. By contrast, units of output before q^* raise more revenue than their

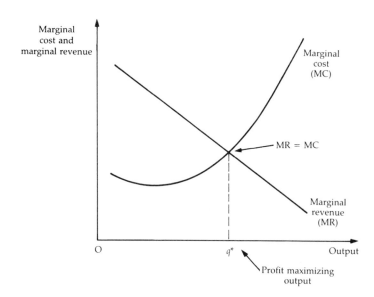

Figure 3.4 Profit-maximizing output

extra costs. Clearly, then, profits are maximized at output q^* where marginal cost equals marginal revenue.

Comparing marginal cost and marginal revenue is vital in deciding whether it pays to *increase* or *reduce* current output. It does not on its own, however, clarify whether the *total* production is profitable. To know this we need to calculate profit over the entire, not just the marginal, output range. One way of doing this is to compare total revenue with total cost. Another way, used here, is to compare price (average revenue) with average total cost. Multiplying the difference by the total output gives, of course, the total profit or loss.

In Figure 3.5 it will be seen that provided the price per unit is above P_1, price exceeds the average total cost (ATC) of production and hence profits are made. These profits are described as *supernormal* (or *pure*) profits as opposed to *normal* profits. This follows from the need for ATC to include the opportunity cost of the capital invested (i.e. the best return that could be earned elsewhere). Thus profit which *just* covers this opportunity cost is called a *normal* profit. Any profit above this is, therefore, *supernormal* profit. If price is between P_1 and P_2, although profits are not made, the price exceeds the average variable costs and hence a contribution is made towards the fixed overhead costs (AFC). Should the price be below

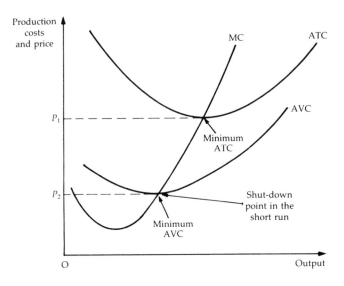

Figure 3.5   The production decision

P_2, then the firm is not covering its variable costs (AVC) and, if this is likely to be more than a very temporary situation, the firm would be well advised to shut down. Continuing in production, given that the variable costs are not being met, must mean a higher loss than if no production occurred at all.

Assuming the firm is in business to make profits, in the long run when all factors of production are variable in supply, whether the firm continues producing depends on whether it makes profits or not. In other words, the revenue earned must cover *all* costs, i.e. price must exceed average total cost. In the long run the concept of diminishing returns is not relevant since it relates to a situation in which at least one factor of production is in fixed supply. With all factors of production variable the firm can change its *scale* of production. This could involve shutting down one plant (with a certain cost structure and associated marginal and average cost curves) and opening up another plant (with its own set of short-run cost relationships). In other words, there is a particular cost structure for production in the short term (the operating period) for each scale of output. A discussion of the nature of production costs in the long run requires an appreciation of *economies* and *diseconomies of scale*.

Economies and diseconomies of scale

In the long run, management decisions will be concerned with how production costs change as the size of the business alters. Opening up new factories, offices and shops is associated with a change in the scale of output. There are broadly three possibilities as follows which may arise:

- **Constant returns to scale.** This arises when the volume of output increases in the same proportion to the volume of inputs.
- **Increasing returns to scale.** This arises where the volume of output rises more quickly than the volume of inputs.
- **Decreasing returns to scale.** This arises where the volume of output rises less quickly than the volume of inputs.

These three possibilities are associated with constant cost, decreasing cost and increasing cost production in the long run respectively. For example, increasing returns to scale should result in decreasing costs (whether or not costs do in fact fall also depends on input prices).

The existence of increasing and decreasing returns to scale is explained by the presence of both *internal* and *external economies* and *diseconomies of scale* in production.

Internal economies of scale

Internal economies of scale arise in industries such as chemicals, oil extraction, High Street banking, etc., where there must be a large output to minimize long-run average costs. Economies stem from the more effective use of available resources resulting in higher productivity and lower costs. A number of internal economies of scale can be readily identified in relation to the following:

- **Labour.** Better use may be made of specialized labour and managerial skills in large firms and there may be economies in training costs. Also, by offering better career prospects large firms can often attract and fully utilize better quality staff. In addition, a superior division of labour may be achievable, which is likely to lead to the development of expertise on the part of staff and a consequent growth in overall productivity.

- **Investment**. There is likely to be a minimum level of investment which is viable in many businesses – a firm cannot buy half of a computer even though it may only require that much computing capacity! Investment economies of scale are likely to be more evident in large- rather than small-scale enterprises.

- **Procurement**. Large firms have muscle and are more likely to be able to gain cost savings through bulk purchasing. This is particularly evident in grocery retailing, for example in the United Kingdom where the market is dominated by a small number of supermarket chains, namely Tesco, Sainsbury, Gateway, ASDA and Argyle (Safeway and Presto) which are able to exercise considerable bargaining power over grocery producers. A firm which purchases all or most of a supplier's output will be able to exert considerable *monopsony* (i.e. dominant buyer) power and drive down price.

- **Research and development**. In industries such as aerospace and pharmaceuticals the pursuit of competitive advantage requires heavy investment in R&D. To be viable, the cost must be spread over the very large output which only large-scale enterprises can hope to achieve.

- **Capital**. Large firms can often raise loan finance more easily and cheaply than smaller businesses since they usually offer greater security to lenders. Also, many larger firms are publicly quoted and hence have access to the equity market.

- **Diversification**. Many large firms spread risk by operating in a number of different markets. For example, ICI supplies paints, fertilizers, pharmaceuticals and so on. A collapse of one market should not, therefore, jeopardize the whole company.

- **Promotion**. Large firms are likely to be able to make more effective use of advertising, specialist sales forces and distribution channels.

- **Transport and distribution**. Only firms producing a large output are likely to be able to employ economically their own transport fleet or be able to negotiate preferential rates with haulage companies (monopsony power again).

- **By-products**. In large enterprises such as oil companies, the opportunity exists to produce a wide range of by-products in quantities which are commercially exploitable.

External economies of scale

Internal economies of scale relate to the operations and decisions made by the individual firm. They are therefore directly under the control of the firm's management. In contrast, external economies arise at the industry level and are generally associated with growth over time in the industry. Three main types of external economies may arise relating to the following:

- **Labour force**. Where firms in an industry group together there is often a large and skilled labour force in the locality which all firms can utilize.

- **Suppliers**. As an industry grows, it is often the case that specialized ancillary firms become concentrated in the locality, supplying components, transport, consultancy services, etc. For example, with the development of the financial services industry in London, it is not surprising that there is also a concentration of accountancy and legal advisory services (as well as wine bars!).

- **Social infrastructure**. A concentration of industry in a particular area will also lead to the development of educational and training facilities, roads, rail networks and a greater availability of housing for workers, all of which may help to reduce industry's costs. Indeed industry and government often co-operate to ensure that these facilities are developed in areas of business expansion, e.g. through new town developments and regional expansion schemes.

Internal diseconomies of scale

A growing firm is likely to benefit from economies of scale which are internal to its operations. However, as growth continues a point may be reached where certain internal *diseconomies* of scale arise. These result in rising long-run marginal and unit costs. Once this occurs the firm needs to consider whether or not further expansion is desirable. Such diseconomies may relate to the following:

- **Management**. The larger a firm's operations become, the more complex the managerial structure often needs to be. There is a danger that management will become bureaucratic and unresponsive. This leads to 'organizational slack' and the internal decision-making process slows down as staff become alienated.

The firm may also become less responsive to changes in the external market. How often do we hear the criticism that a firm has 'too many layers of management' resulting from inadequately managed growth?

- **Labour.** It is a well-known fact that industrial disputes are more likely to occur in large rather than small companies. This arises because, as the labour force grows, the gap between 'management' and 'the workers' grows and consequently loyalty to the firm falls. At the same time unionization increases and this can bring with it more rigid wage-bargaining processes leading to friction between management and workforce. Costs may rise because of lowered productivity and the need for greater managerial supervision. Absenteeism and slacking in work also tend to be more prevalent in large firms.

- **Other inputs.** As the firm grows its demand for inputs increases. If the supply of these inputs is limited then their unit cost will rise as the firm's output expands. This applies not only to materials and components but to certain skilled labour requirements.

External diseconomies of scale

Sometimes costs rise as the whole industry expands in a particular area. Growth can put pressure on the price of housing and transport and this may ultimately feed through to higher wage demands and increased distribution costs. There may also be additional costs associated with congestion and other environmental hazards.

Production costs in the long run

As firms expand production over the long run and move to different scales of operation, if internal and external economies of scale exist unit costs will fall as the volume of output increases. This represents *increasing returns to scale* or decreasing cost production as defined above. Presumably, however, unit costs will not always decline (otherwise they would eventually approach zero) and hence we would expect them eventually to level out. The firm is then said to operate under constant cost production. It is conceivable that at some very large output internal and external diseconomies of scale might cause unit costs to rise, leading to increasing cost production. These three possibilities – increasing, constant and decreasing returns to scale are illustrated in Figure 3.6.

The art of good management is to capture the benefits of internal and external economies and, of course, to avoid the onset of internal and external diseconomies. Ideally, firms will want to operate at the level of output which corresponds to minimum unit costs over the long run or what is sometimes termed the *minimum efficient scale* (MES). This represents the technical optimum scale of production for the firm. In Figure 3.6, an output of at least q_1 must be achieved to minimize long-run average costs and hence this is the MES. As there is constant cost production between outputs q_1 and q_2 there is no *single* optimum scale – instead, any of the outputs in this range represents a technical optimum. However, if the long-run average cost curve were U-shaped there would be *one* scale of output, at the bottom of the U, which represented the technical optimum. Achieving MES gives a firm a strong competitive advantage in the market place over higher-cost producers.

Clearly, management must strive to avoid long-run average costs rising. As one of the major diseconomies of large-scale production is managerial breakdown, firms have tended to establish sub-units, separate operating companies and so on to avoid this. This gives rise to what is often called an 'M-form' (multi-form) structure in which parts of the company operate with considerable managerial inde-

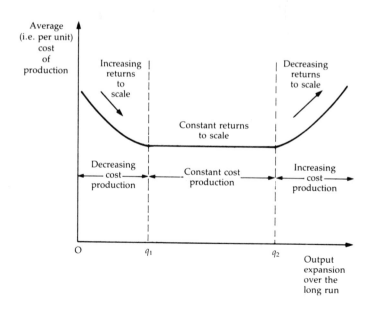

Figure 3.6 The long-run average cost curve

pendence, especially in terms of day-to-day decision-making. This reduces bureaucracy and speeds up decisions. The most extreme example of this is where a holding company is set up (e.g. Hanson Trust). In this case a small number of senior managers and support staff seek to co-ordinate and oversee the activities of the much larger subsidiary companies. In contrast, smaller firms tend to be managed more from the centre through a clear managerial hierarchy and with little decentralized decision-making. This structure is often referred to as a 'U-form' (unitary form) structure and makes sense where tight control must be imposed from the centre on day-to-day operations. Figure 3.7 highlights the key features of the M-form and U-form organizational structures.

Other ways in which firms attempt to avoid the onset of

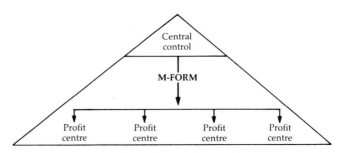

Flattened managerial pyramid

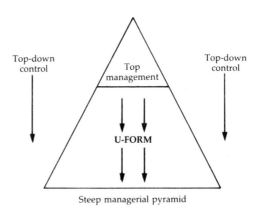

Steep managerial pyramid

Figure 3.7 Organizational structures

diseconomies of scale may involve one or more of the following decisions:

- **Relocation of operations** which are inexpensive and which may be at the lower end of the added-value scale, e.g. Japanese electronics and car companies moving assembly operations out of Japan to avoid costs associated with congestion and labour shortages; UK companies moving from the south-east to the north.
- **Contracting-out** of certain services (e.g. catering, computing), and *divestment* (selling-off of low-profit activities).
- **Reorganizing the management structure** (e.g. the 'flattening' of the managerial pyramid by UK companies such as BP and BT in the early 1990s).
- **Introduction of new or improved technology** to increase productivity in production and to improve management systems; as illustrated in Figure 3.8 this leads to a downward shift in the long-run average cost curve since a given volume of output can now be produced at lower unit costs.

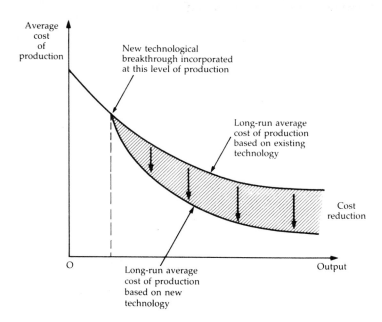

Figure 3.8 The impact of improved technology on long-run production costs

The experience curve

Economies and diseconomies of scale relate to the behaviour of long-run production costs as the *scale* of output changes. It is also likely that unit costs will fall over time as experience of producing and selling a good or service increases. In other words, costs of production decline as the *cumulative volume* of output rises.

Figure 3.9 provides an example of a typical *experience curve*. By combining the notion of costs related to scale and experience, we can conclude that the achievement of competitive advantage through lower costs than competitors' lies in growth of production, which in turn implies (at least in a relatively static market) capturing a larger market share. Indeed we can see how a 'virtuous circle' could build up in which lower unit costs enhance competitiveness, drive up market share and permit a further cost-reducing expansion in output due to economies of scale and experience curve effects as illustrated in Figure 3.10.

Equally, a loss of competitive advantage leading to a fall in market share can cut demand, reduce output and force up unit costs leading to a 'vicious circle' of competitive decline.

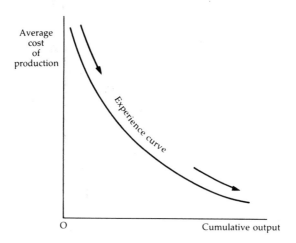

Figure 3.9 The experience curve

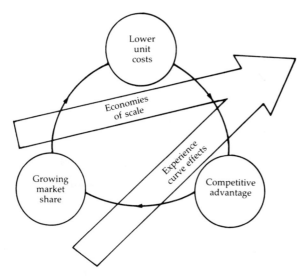

Figure 3.10 The 'virtuous circle'

Optimal scale and x-inefficiency

Companies may not always be able to identify exactly their short-run or long-run technical optimum, as this requires considerable knowledge of the nature of production costs as output rises. Even in the presence of complete information there may not always, of course, be sufficient demand for the firm's product to justify increasing output to reach the optimal long-run scale of production. Companies' unit costs may be higher than is technically feasible – a 'production-cost' gap – for the following two broad reasons:

1. The firm is not producing at its optimal scale of production.
2. The firm wastes resources and its costs are higher than necessary at its *existing* scale of production (so-called 'x-inefficiency' because it can exist to any degree). Remember that so far we have been assuming that the firm uses its resources efficiently – there is no waste or slack in the business.

Four possible situations are illustrated in Figure 3.11. These show the following:

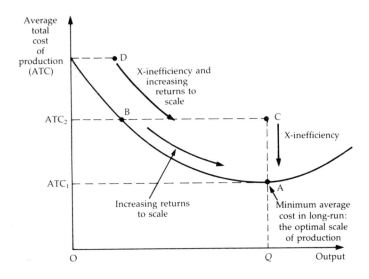

Figure 3.11 The 'production-cost' gap

1. A firm at point A on its long-run average cost curve is operating at the optimal scale of output where unit costs are minimized. In addition, it is operating at maximum efficiency in terms of avoiding waste of resources – it is on its long-run average cost curve which represents the minimum cost of producing at any output (there is no x-inefficiency present).

2. A firm at point B could reduce its unit costs by increasing its scale of output. Once again, however, as the firm is operating on the achievable long-run average cost curve there is no x-inefficiency. In other words, while firm B is not operating at its most efficient scale of production, it is nevertheless doing the best it can given its existing capacity.

3. A firm at point C is operating at its optimal scale of production but its unit costs are higher than could be achieved if efficiency was maximized. Costs could be lowered to point A by reducing waste or organizational slack. The difference between C and A is the x-inefficiency gap for this firm.

4. Management of a firm at a point such as D have the greatest challenge of all – and the firm is at the greatest risk of failure! It is not cost efficient in terms of using the available resources (it is not operating on its long-run average cost curve). Also, it is failing to take full advantage of economies of scale (it is

producing below optimal scale). Not to mince words, the firm has the potential to move from D to A, and if this potential is not recognized by the current management, then it ought to be taken over by new management!

Since x-inefficiency represents a waste of resources, a function of management is to minimize it. Some economists argue that x-inefficiency is a very common phenomenon, especially in state-owned companies where the profit motive does not exist and hence the drive for efficiency may be reduced. In terms of private sector joint-stock companies, the shareholders (the owners or 'principals' of the firm) appoint directors as their 'agents' to manage the firm efficiently – an agent–principal relationship exists. This raises the whole question of the objectives of firms and management, which we address at length in Chapter 5. Profit maximization and hence the drive for a more efficient use of resources, though presumably desired by shareholders, may not always be the primary goal of managers – some managers may seek glory in being in charge of a worldwide company, with the discretion to hire and fire and with responsibility for large sums of discretionary expenditure. The pursuit of such goals may lead to inefficiency in private sector firms. It is suggested, however, that the threat of takeover by new management, alongside the need to sell products in competitive markets, should limit x-inefficiency in the private sector; though the extent to which this threat does effectively constrain non-profit behaviour is the subject of on-going debate.

The firm's supply curve

So far we have looked at the relationship between a firm's volume of production and its costs. Ultimately, of course, the volume actually sold depends on the price which consumers are willing to pay for the product, which in conjunction with the costs of production determines profit. We now examine the relationship between costs, supply and the market price. This gives rise to the following concepts:

- The supply curve, and
- elasticity of supply.

Deriving the firm's supply curve

For a firm in a highly competitive industry, the supply curve shows the amount that it is willing to supply at all possible market prices (just as the demand curve shows how much consumers are willing to buy at each price). In general, the higher the price the more the firm will be willing to supply, for two reasons. First, a higher price may mean more profit. Secondly, in many cases, especially in the short run, the marginal cost of production increases as supply rises, hence a higher price is needed to cover the higher costs. The actual extra amount produced will depend upon the marginal cost of producing the extra output. Hence the firm's supply curve in a very competitive industry is traced out by its marginal cost curve, as illustrated in Figure 3.12. Since, as explained earlier, a profit-maximizing firm should not produce if price is below the average variable cost of production, it is the marginal cost curve above the firm's average variable cost curve which is the firm's supply curve. This is given by the curve AB in Figure 3.12, showing the output that the firm would be willing to supply at various prices, P_1, P_2, P_3, etc.

It is important to note that strictly the supply curve can only be derived for firms operating in very competitive environments. Where competition is restricted, as in the extreme case of a single

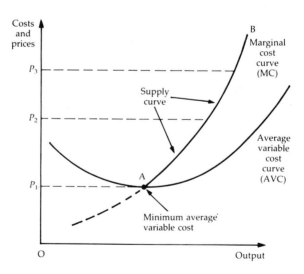

Figure 3.12 Deriving the supply curve for a firm in a competitive
environment

firm monopoly, the profit-maximizing firm will set its price *above* its marginal costs of production, as explained in Chapter 4. Therefore, in these markets the concept of a 'supply curve' as defined above is inappropriate. A monopoly firm is not at the mercy of the market like a competitive firm; it does not have to take the market price as given and react to it. On the contrary, the management have the power to select the price–sales combination on their demand curve that they prefer so as to maximize profit. The monopoly firm is therefore a price-maker not a price-taker. This does not mean, however, that the monopolist can increase price indefinitely since consumer demand will always be affected by price. The relationship between price and supply in markets where competition is highly restricted should become clearer on reading Chapter 4.

Conditions of supply

Of course, price is not the only factor that affects the decision to supply even in highly competitive markets. The other factors likely to impact upon the supply decision are referred to as the *conditions of supply*. Important examples of these other factors are the following:

- **Changes in costs of production**. These include changes in the costs of labour, raw materials, capital charges and the impact of new technology on costs, all of which may impact on the balance between labour and capital intensive production and ultimately profitability. For example, when the price of oil rose in the 1970s, a number of industries dependent upon oil as a major energy source were forced to retrench.

- **Prices of other products**. As the prices of other products alter, the firm may decide to switch production. For example, in farming a decline in dairy product revenues in Europe has led to a switch to other products such as rape seed.

- **Changes in profit expectations**. Between times of boom and slump, profit expectations can change dramatically leading to a reassessment of business strategy, e.g. in the early 1990s in the depressed UK housing market a number of property companies withdrew from new developments.

- **Climate**. Climate is obviously important to supply decisions in industries such as farming, building, insurance, transport and travel.

As any of the conditions of supply change, firms will tend to supply more or less of their products at any given price. In terms of Figure 3.13, this is equivalent to a shift in the supply curve. A favourable change in supply conditions, e.g. reduced costs of production, will shift the curve (S_1S_1) to the right (to S_2S_2) as more can now be supplied profitably at any given price, whereas an unfavourable change in conditions, e.g. storm damage to productive capacity, will cause the supply curve to shift sharply to the left (to S_3S_3). One important function of management is to monitor how supply conditions are altering and are *likely to alter* in the near future in relevant markets. It is important to business success to anticipate favourable and unfavourable changes which are likely to impact on production and ultimately profitability.

Elasticity of supply

Just as in Chapter 2 we saw that the responsiveness of consumer demand to changes in price could be measured, so we can also

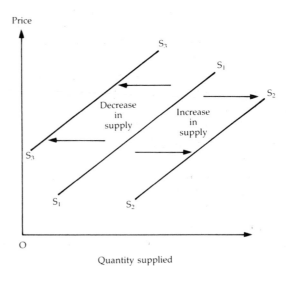

Figure 3.13 Shifting the firm's supply curve

measure how supply responds to a price change. This gives rise to the concept of *elasticity of supply* (E_s), which is defined as:

$$E_s = \frac{\text{percentage change in the quantity supplied}}{\text{percentage change in price}}$$

The numerical value of E_s will always be positive. A figure of more than 1 suggests that the supply is relatively responsive to price changes. In other words, when a product's price rises or falls there is a more than proportional change in the amount supplied. For instance, if a 10% price rise is accompanied by a 15% increase in supply, supply in this case is said to be *elastic* – the elasticity equals 1.5. When the supply response to a price change is less than proportionate, i.e. less than 1, supply is said to be relatively *inelastic*. For example, if price fell by 4%, but the firm chose to reduce its supply only by 1%, the supply is inelastic – the elasticity is 0.25. It is conceivable that a firm's supply might change exactly in proportion to the change in price, a situation referred to as one of *unit* price elasticity.

The sort of factors which tend to influence the elasticity of supply include the extent to which production costs change as supply is altered; the existence of spare capacity; the extent to which the firm carries stocks; and the extent to which the firm can switch capacity from or to alternative productions. Ultimately, the responsiveness of supply has a time dimension – the longer the period the firm has to adapt to the price change, then the more elastic (responsive) supply is likely to be. In the very short run, of course, it may not be possible for a firm to change its supply at all. In which case supply is said to be perfectly inelastic (it has a zero price elasticity). Figure 3.14 gives examples of supply elasticities.

Concluding remarks

On first reading, much of what has been included in this chapter may appear to managers as fairly esoteric and far removed from the real world of harsh decision-making. But nothing could be further from the truth. The cost concepts introduced are fundamental to any

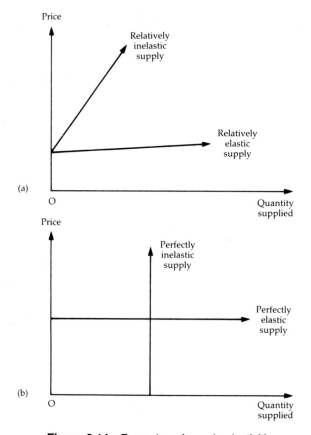

Figure 3.14   Examples of supply elasticities

analysis of actual business operations, for the extent to which costs change as output varies has obvious implications for pricing and competitiveness. A successful competitive strategy cannot be developed in isolation from a full appreciation of the firm's cost structure. Moreover, the nature of the firm's costs must have an important bearing on longer-run decisions regarding whether to consolidate, expand capacity, cut back production, and ultimately whether to shut down. Operational and planning decisions can only be based on a clear picture of the changing nature of the cost structure facing the firm.

In the next two chapters we build on the foundations established in this and the previous chapter on consumer demand. We turn first to consider the different types of competitive environment that firms may face and the appropriate strategies they may adopt.

4

The competitive environment

The essence of the competitive environment

This chapter is concerned with one of the most important factors that impinges on the behaviour and performance of a firm, namely the competitive environment in which it operates. The extent of competition a firm faces has implications, in particular, for the pricing of products, the output supplied and hence the level of investment and employment, the stability of sales, the pace of innovation, the marketing of products and ultimately the profits earned.

As outlined in Chapter 1, economists distinguish between the following four broad forms of competition:

- **Perfect competition**: this is concerned with very competitive markets.
- **Monopoly**: this is concerned with markets in which there is only one supplier.
- **Monopolistic competition**: this form arises where there are many suppliers but of slightly differentiated products.
- **Oligopoly**: this is concerned with markets where there are a few large suppliers usually of branded products.

Each of these market forms is discussed in detail below and the lessons for management are identified.

Competitive strategy

Today, most firms operate in a number of different markets. An electrical goods supplier such as Amstrad in the United Kingdom supplies computers, satellite dishes, video recorders and camcorders, to name but some of its major products. ICI produces a large range of outputs for the bulk chemicals and pharmaceuticals markets. Hanson Trust acts as a holding company with a highly diversified set of subsidiaries supplying a wide range of consumer markets. Therefore it is a major abstraction to talk about *a firm* and *its market*. Firms are usually made up of a number of business units with different products aimed at different markets. Equally, the notion of an industry runs into similar difficulties when analyzing competition. It can be difficult to define the boundaries of an industry. BMW and Lada are major operators in the world car industry, but they are not competitors in any meaningful sense. Competition is ultimately defined by consumers' perceptions – does the consumer see the firms' products as substitutes when making expenditure decisions? A substitute is something the consumer perceives as meeting the same need.

Competition may not simply be a battle for consumers confined to the boundaries of one industry. In other words, when identifying the competitive market, traditional definitions of the firm and the industry may be quite inadequate. For companies operating in different markets the term 'firm' as used below can be best understood as a business unit. Therefore, that part of an electronics company which sells compact disc players is a separate business unit or firm from another part of the company which might supply television sets, video recorders, etc. In some circumstances it may be useful to narrow the definition further, say to the business unit which supplies 'up-market' CD players solely to the United States.

Substitution is the key to competition and one way of expressing this, as we saw in Chapter 2, is in terms of *cross-price elasticity*. Cross-price elasticity of demand relates the change in demand for one product to a change in the price of another product. Where products are readily substitutable by consumers, there will be a relatively *high* and *positive* cross-price elasticity. Thus the prosperity of a glass bottle manufacturer may be affected less by other members of the glass industry (companies in the industry which do not manufacture bottles are of no significance) and more by producers of alternative drinks containers, namely metal can and plastic bottle suppliers.

Only after the nature of the competition is defined and the market clarified can a worthwhile *competitive strategy* be developed, because only then does it become clear what level and type of competition exists. There is no point in the management of BMW shaping their strategy until it is clear *who* are the competitors and what is the precise *nature and scope* of the competition.

Competitive strategy is concerned with how management contends with the competitive environment it identifies.

The first stage is to identify the competition faced and the second to determine what policies should be adopted to steal a competitive advantage over other producers in the market (how should the firm *position* itself in the market?). If BMW identifies Mercedes, Jaguar, Audi, Saab, Alfa Romeo and Rover as its major competition in Europe, on what does competition centre? This requires a profile of the typical consumer and the nature of the consumer demand, using the principles of consumer behaviour introduced in Chapter 2. How is the typical consumer choosing between these suppliers – to what extent is the decision based on price or other product attributes such as build quality, longevity, reliability, fuel and servicing economy and performance? For example, if most potential BMW buyers rate reliability highly in their purchase decision, skimping on build quality so as to reduce production costs and lower price would be disastrous for the BMW motor company.

Market research suggests that for many products today quality is rated at least as highly and often more highly than price by consumers. If this were not so then East European car and electronics manufacturers would have seen off the competition in Western markets years ago! In Chapter 6 we look in detail at the 'marketing mix' in which price is but one variable in the consumer's decision to buy, but in this chapter we will concentrate mainly on price. We shall also assume that firms attempt to maximize their profits in the short run. Hence, they alter prices and outputs with a view to raising immediate profitability. This may not be realistic. Firms may place more emphasis in the short run on achieving high market share and postponing high profits until they are dominant in the market. In some cases, even long-run profit maximization may not be the objective. The subject of management objectives is discussed in detail in Chapter 5.

We turn first to a consideration of the economists' four generic market models noted above – perfect competition, monopoly, monopolistic competition and oligopoly. The degree of competition a firm actually faces varies depending where on the *competitive spectrum* it lies. Figure 4.1 illustrates this spectrum which runs from pure monopoly to perfect competition, with monopolistic competition and oligopoly nearer the middle. Hence, firm A is in a more competitive market than firm B, which itself faces more competition than firm C. Firm C is closest to being a monopolist. At an early phase in establishing a competitive strategy it is important for management to decide where on this spectrum their businesses lie (bearing in mind that a firm may operate in various markets and therefore more than one position on the spectrum may be relevant).

Each of the economists' market models is a theoretical construct designed as an abstraction of actual markets. Each is based on a set of restrictive assumptions and none is designed to *describe* a real-world market. Since every market has its own idiosyncrasies it would be impossible to provide a descriptive model for every market! Like other economists' models, they are constructed so that certain *predictions* can be made which have general application. Although abstract in nature, each of these market models provides important insights into the functioning of real-world markets. Before proceeding to read the remainder of this chapter it might be useful to review the discussion of demand, revenue and cost curves in Chapters 2 and 3. The models outlined in this chapter directly employ the concepts introduced in those chapters.

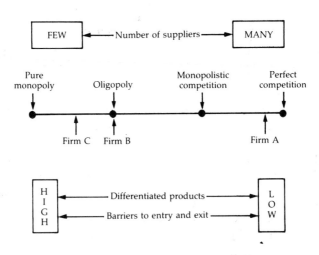

Figure 4.1 The competitive spectrum

Perfect competition

A perfectly competitive market is one in which there is an extremely high degree of competition. Bearing in mind that it is ultimately the consumer who defines competition, this implies a very large number of perfect substitutes in the market. Strictly, perfect competition requires the following conditions:

- Homogeneous (identical) products.
- No firm with a cost advantage – all firms have identical cost curves.
- A very large number of suppliers – no single producer by varying its output can perceptibly affect the total market output and hence the market price.
- Free entry into and exit from the industry – competition is sustained over time.
- No transport and distribution costs to distort competition.
- Suppliers and consumers who are fully informed about profits, prices and the characteristics of products in the market – hence ignorance does not distort competition.

A market which comes closest to exhibiting all of these conditions is the stock market. Any particular stock is homogeneous, there is plenty of readily available information (e.g. published prices), transaction costs are relatively low, buyers and sellers can readily enter and leave the market and individual buyers and sellers of stock usually have an insignificant effect on price.

Unregulated commodity markets are also highly, if not perfectly, competitive. For example, in an unregulated world coffee market, the consumer might distinguish Brazilian coffee from coffee from other parts of the world but not the coffee from a particular Brazilian estate. If this is so, from the consumer's perspective Brazilian coffee is a homogeneous product. Hence, the price of Brazilian coffee on the world market determines the price received by the individual Brazilian coffee grower. The individual grower is a *price-taker*. The grower cannot set his price independently of the other growers. Competition drives prices down to a minimum level and if a single grower decides to raise his price consumers will switch to alternative suppliers.

In perfectly competitive markets because the product is homogeneous the competition can only centre on price. The demand curve faced by a producer is therefore horizontal or *perfectly price elastic* (see pp. 28–34 for a discussion of price elasticity). The way in which a perfectly competitive market operates can be best described with the aid of diagrams. We will stay with the Brazilian coffee example. In Figure 4.2 diagram (a) relates to the overall market and shows the demand (DD) and supply (SS) of Brazilian coffee. Diagram (b) shows the short-run marginal and average total cost curves (MC and ATC) and marginal and average revenue curves (MR and AR) for one of the coffee growers. Assuming that each grower has the same cost structure, the revenue and cost curves in diagram (b) reflect the position for any of the growers.

The total supply of Brazilian coffee and the world demand for it sets a market price for coffee of P_1 (shown in diagram (a)). This means that each grower must sell at that price. The firm can supply varying amounts of coffee but must sell it at price P_1. Since the price and therefore the average revenue are constant, the marginal revenue is also constant and equal to the average revenue and price. Also, let us assume that the cost curves include a *normal* profit to reflect the opportunity cost of capital (i.e. what the capital in the production activity could earn if invested in the next best alternative investment). Any additional profit above and beyond this is referred to as *supernormal* or pure profit. To achieve maximum profit, the

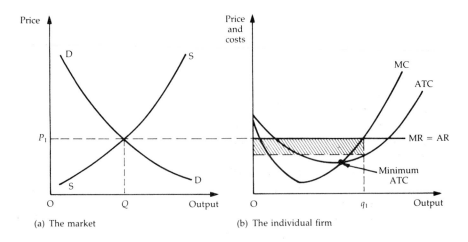

(a) The market   (b) The individual firm

Figure 4.2 Perfect competition: short-run equilibrium

individual grower will aim to supply q_1 where MR = MC (why this is the maximum-profit output is explained in detail in Chapter 3, pages 50–2). At this output, the pure profit earned per unit of output is shown by the distance between the AR and ATC curves (hence the total supernormal profit is the hatched area).

The existence of pure profit now acts as an incentive for new growers to enter the market. But as new suppliers enter and produce coffee, the total market supply must rise and, assuming that market demand is not also increasing, price will fall. This will continue until the pure profit disappears and there is no incentive for further farmers to switch to growing coffee beans. At this time, the market stabilizes or reaches a *long-run equilibrium*.

This process is illustrated in Figure 4.3. The increase in the market supply of coffee is shown by a shift to the right in the supply curve in diagram (a), while the effect on the output, price and profits of growers already in the market is shown in diagram (b). The market reaches equilibrium (at a price, P_2, which is below the original price, P_1) when AR equates to long-run ATC and hence pure profit no longer exists. If for some reason the market price of coffee should fall further in the future, then coffee growers would make less than a normal profit; consequently some would leave the business and switch to other crops. As they leave, the market supply would fall and in time the price would recover sufficiently so that normal profits were earned again. Therefore, whenever in a perfectly competitive market firms earn more than or less than normal profits, in the long run normal profit is restored through the entry and exit

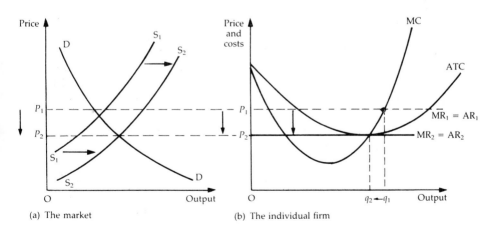

Figure 4.3 Perfect competition: long-run equilibrium

of suppliers. It follows that free entry and exit of suppliers is critical to the operation of a highly competitive market.

To summarize, under perfect competition:

- in the short run, until the entry or exit of sufficient firms occurs, pure profit or losses can exist;
- in the long run, once the process of market adjustment is complete, only a normal profit is earned.

Thus perfect competition drives profits down to a normal level and provides consumers with low-priced products. Also, firms operate at optimal scale in the long run. This is apparent in Figure 4.3(b) where production occurs at the output at which the long-run average cost curve is at its minimum.

Monopoly

Monopoly is the polar opposite of perfect competition. Economists define a monopolist as the *sole* supplier to a particular market. This should not be confused with the everyday use of the term to describe a supplier with a relatively large share of the market. Nor should it be confused with monopoly as defined in government legislation – in the United Kingdom a supplier with more than 25% of the market. Like the perfect competition model, the monopoly model is designed to be an extreme case and it is rarely found in practice. Commonly, state industries are described as monopolies, but though they often dominate an *industry*, they are rarely monopolies of a *market*. In other words, it is possible to find examples of monopolistic industries, but rarely of monopolistic markets. This is a good illustration of the point that competition is in the eyes of the consumer. For instance, in the United Kingdom British Coal controls most domestic coal production, but it faces competition from imported coal and from other energy sources, namely oil, electricity and gas. Similarly, British Rail owns the UK rail network, but its market is transport. The management of BR wrestle daily with competition from coach services, airlines and private cars.

The monopoly model allows us to make predictions about the

kind of behaviour we would tend to find in markets where competition is severely restricted. Since the monopoly firm is the sole supplier, its supply is the market supply. The demand (average revenue) curve facing the monopolist will be downward sloping implying that more can be sold at a lower price. Thus the marginal revenue curve is also downward sloping (for an explanation of the precise relationship between the AR and MR curves, see page 38). Assuming once again that maximum profit is the objective, in Figure 4.4 the firm should supply output q_1 as this is the output where MR = MC. This supply would be sold at price P_1, as indicated by the demand curve with a unit cost equal to C_1. With once again a normal profit included in the costs of production, this price–output configuration produces a pure profit per unit shown by the distance between the AR and ATC curves at output q_1. Hence total profit is once again the hatched area.

If this was a competitive market new entrants would enter the industry and price would fall until the pure profit had been competed away, as described earlier. Monopolists, however, are able to preserve their market because of *barriers to entry* (otherwise they would cease to be monopolists). Barriers to entry prevent

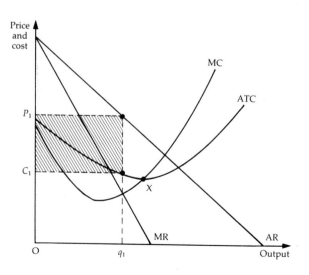

Figure 4.4 Monopoly

competitors entering the market. Important examples are the following:

- Patents and copyright (e.g. the patent for instant cameras held by Polaroid which excluded competition; IBM's patent which prevented other firms entering the golfball typewriter market).
- Government regulations, licenses and nationalization statutes (e.g. the monopoly rights over certain letter deliveries held by national post offices).
- Tariffs and non-tariff barriers against imports.
- The existence of *natural monopolies*. Natural monopoly exists where more than one supplier leads to an appreciable rise in unit costs, e.g. in electricity transmission. This could be because of economies of scale in the production of one product or so-called *economies of scope*, which arise from cost savings associated with producing a range of products together.
- Lower costs of production than competitors because of know-how (experience economies).
- Control of necessary factors of production. Until the 1940s the Aluminium Company of America controlled almost every source of bauxite, the raw material used to produce aluminium, and therefore monopolized the production of the commodity in the United States.
- The need for high capital investment to match the size and costs of the monopolist, the cost of which cannot be recouped if the firm leaves the industry (so-called 'sunk costs'). For example, plant and machinery may be specific to that industry and therefore cannot be used elsewhere or sold so as to recoup the written down value. Sunk costs make investing to compete with the monopolist much riskier.
- Control of distribution channels, e.g. breweries owning tied houses, that is to say, outlets through which they have sole or privileged rights to sell their beer.

Even where there is no absolute barrier to entry, the monopolist may be able to *deter* competitors by, for example:

- Predatory pricing or the threat of a price war and other action against potential competitors.
- Creating excess capacity, which signals to potential suppliers that the monopolist might react to competition by increasing output and thus reducing the market price.

- Creating brand loyalty, including large-scale advertising expenditure.

- High research and development expenditure, as in the pharmaceuticals industry.

Given the lack of competition, monopoly is associated with the following:

- **Higher prices, higher profits and lower outputs than under perfect competition.** In a highly competitive market price is set equal to marginal cost. The monopolist, however, prices above marginal cost leading to a higher price and a smaller output. This is illustrated in Figure 4.5 where, for simplicity, constant cost production is assumed (MC = ATC). The profit-maximizing competitive firm sets its price according to marginal cost and hence charges a price of P_c and supplies q_c. In contrast, the monopolist sells output q_m at the higher price of P_m and earns large profits shown by the hatched area.

- **A loss of consumer welfare.** The consumer has no choice in the market place. Also, remember from Chapter 2 that the area under the demand curve can be taken to represent *consumer surplus* (utility obtained by the consumer over and above the price he or she paid for the product). With the competitive price and output the consumer surplus in Figure 4.5 is given by the triangular area aP_cb. Under monopoly it is the smaller area aP_me. Part of the competitive consumer surplus has been transferred to the monopolist as additional profit (area P_mefP_c), while the area efb is called *deadweight loss*. In other words, monopoly has led to a net loss of welfare equal to the area efb, while a further part of the benefit received by consumers in the competitive market (area P_mefP_c) is now transferred to the monopoly supplier in the form of supernormal profit.

- **Higher costs.** Where costs are not constant as output changes (the usual case) the profit-maximizing monopolist does not produce at technically optimum scale. The minimum point on the ATC curve (point X in Figure 4.4) involves an output which is different to that at which profits are maximized. Also, the lack of competition may lead to waste or x-inefficiency (for an explanation of x-inefficiency see pages 61–3), which means higher costs of production at *all* outputs. Monopolies tend to be sleepy giants. Confirmation for this has recently come from Eastern Europe, where following the collapse of communism

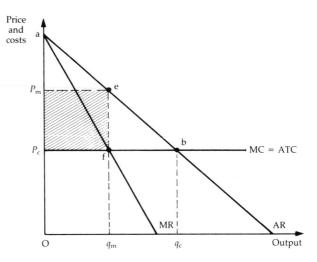

Figure 4.5 The welfare costs of monopoly

state monopolies have been forced to compete for the first time. For example, in former East Germany the sole and state-owned travel agent, Europäisches Reisebüro, following German unification had to face competition from over 300 newly formed and privately run agencies. An immediate consequence was a loss of one-quarter of its workforce and the sale of one-third of its outlets. In the United Kingdom, BT, formerly a government monopoly supplier of telecommunications, is threatened by the growth of its new rival Mercury Communications. Since 1989 BT has announced thousands of redundancies and a major restructuring in an overdue effort to streamline the company.

The inefficiency associated with monopoly has led governments to legislate against them. However, it is possible to conceive of certain circumstances in which monopoly might be advantageous. The clearest example is where there are significant *economies of scale* (or *scope*). As we saw in the previous chapter, economies of scale occur where there are major cost savings if large outputs are produced. These economies might arise in production, investment, research and development, marketing, distribution or management. Returning to Figure 4.5, if significant economies of scale existed then the monopolist's costs would be lower at the profit-maximizing output than the competitive firm's costs (imagine the MC and ATC line shifting downwards). In which case, it is possible for both the monopolist to earn higher profits and the consumer to benefit from lower prices. This could result in *more* consumer surplus than if production had occurred in a competitive industry. Perfect competition is obviously superior to monopoly in terms of low prices to the consumer only when technology allows many suppliers at optimal cost. Also, the profits earned by the monopolist might be ploughed back into more investment and R&D spending to the ultimate benefit of the consumer. Of course, in practice monopoly benefits can easily be frittered away by inefficient management. Nevertheless, there may be dynamic gains from monopoly which the static approach of traditional economic theory overlooks.

The existence of such dynamic gains has led a number of economists in recent years to argue that, provided there are no undue barriers to entry into the industry, governments should not be over-concerned about the existence of monopolies. Where there are no market barriers, dominance must arise from the superior efficiency of the firm in meeting consumer needs. In other words, high profits are a reward for producing the right products. At the same time, monopoly profits act as an incentive for other firms to seek out ways of competing, thus monopolies tend to be transient – a first-mover advantage. As an example of this, Rank Xerox, which first developed the photocopier, earned a 41% rate of return in 1975 but by 1987 this had fallen to 13% because of increased competition.

The existing supplier may have a process patent but perhaps another, and superior, process can be found. Perhaps an alternative product can be made. If it is not possible to get bauxite to manufacture aluminium, why not make products out of steel or plastic? Moreover, provided the barriers to entry and exit are not significant, monopolists will be prone to 'hit and run' competition. Whenever the monopolist earns excessive profits new competitors will enter the market. To prevent this, the monopolist must price his product to reduce the risks of entry. This requires prices equal to long-run average costs so that profits are normal. Thus the monopolist may *act* like a competitive firm whenever its market is *contestable*. Also, the threat of state intervention may be a further limitation on the activities of a monopoly. Most governments have legislation to control monopolies.

If a monopoly arises from organic growth, this implies that it arose because the firm was efficient in meeting consumer needs. However, monopoly achieved by acquisitions and mergers may have been motivated by a desire to limit competition. The implications for government policy are very different. Where a firm is dominant in the market because it meets consumer needs best, arguably the state should not intervene. Instead, governments might be better advised to look to reducing those monopolies that exist because of state controls and nationalization through a programme of deregulation and privatization. We consider the nature of government industrial policy and anti-monopoly legislation further in Chapter 9.

Government regulators have a number of ways in which they can assess the extent of competition in a market. These are discussed below.

Profit rates

In a competitive market profit rates should be lowered. Hence, the level of profitability might be an indicator of the degree of monopolization of the market. In practice, however, a snapshot of current profit rates tells us nothing about how profit rates are *changing* over time in the face of competition. The use of profit rates is therefore a very crude indicator of monopoly power. An alternative is to use what is called the *Lerner index*. Since in very competitive markets prices equal marginal costs, the excess of price over marginal cost can be taken to reflect the extent to which competition is imperfect. The Lerner index is measured as $(P - MC)/P$.

Concentration ratios

These ratios represent the extent of the market supplied by a given number of firms. For example, a four-firm concentration ratio shows the percentage of the market supplied by the four largest producers. Therefore, if the four-firm concentration ratio is 60%, this means that 60% of the market is supplied by the four largest companies. Where the four-firm concentration ratio is 100%, this means that four (or fewer) firms produce all the output and hence the industry is highly concentrated. In addition to four-firm concentration ratios, five-firm and sometimes eight-firm ratios are used by economists.

Market share

Although frequently used to assess the degree of competition in a market, the concentration ratio does not tell us the different market shares of the largest producers. For example, there may be two industries with four-firm concentration ratios of 60%, but in one industry each of the four has 15% of the market, while in the other industry three of the firms have 5% each and a dominant firm has

45% of the market. The amount of competition may be very different in the two markets. We might expect to see more monopolistic behaviour in the latter market where the dominant firm may be more able to affect the market price. An alternative approach to assessing competition is therefore to look at the market share of the largest firms.

Herfindahl Index (HI)

Now commonly used by government bodies when measuring the degree of competition in a market, this index takes into account the *size distribution* of firms. It is measured as:

$$\text{HERFINDAHL INDEX (HI)} = \sum_{i=1}^{n} S_i^2$$

where S_i represents the market shares of each of the i firms in the market. Hence, the index depends on the number of firms in the industry *and* their relative market shares. A value closer to 1 indicates increased monopolization because it suggests a small number of firms and/or very unequal market shares.

Monopolistic competition

The perfect competition and monopoly models have proved useful for predicting behaviour in markets in which there are very large numbers of suppliers or one supplier respectively. Many markets today, however, do not accord with either of these extremes. Perfect competition assumes homogeneous products, but even where there is a large number of suppliers to a market there is often some 'brand loyalty' so that suppliers are not complete price-takers, e.g. in the retail sector or personal services such as hairdressing.

Monopolistic competition refers to markets in which there are a large number of firms competing, supplying products which consumers believe are *close* but not complete substitutes. Therefore, it is a market in which firms compete through slight product differentiation, and management has discretion in pricing, trading off price against quantity sold. The demand curve faced by each firm will be more price elastic because of the existence of considerable competition. It is assumed that there is relatively free entry into and exit from the industry and that entry and exit are regulated by the level of profit earned.

Figure 4.6 illustrates the cost and revenue curves for a typical firm in monopolistic competition. Assuming a goal of profit maximization, the output q_1 is sold (where MR = MC) at price P_1 (note that the price is greater than the marginal cost). By comparing the average revenue curve (AR) and the short-run average cost curve (ATC) we can see that the firm is earning a pure profit. This profit is AR − ATC per unit (i.e. $P_1 - C_1$), which gives a total pure profit once again shown by the hatched area.

This profit can be expected to attract new suppliers into the market. The effect of this is to reduce the demand for the output of the existing firms in the industry and to increase the price sensitivity of their products. The market demand is shared out amongst a larger number of suppliers competing keenly on price. Assuming no impediments to the competitive process, new entry will continue until all of the pure profit is competed away. The effect is shown in Figure 4.7. The demand curve (AR curve) has shifted inwards and become more elastic until it is tangential at the profit-maximizing output to the long-run average cost curve. At output q_2 and price P_2, average revenue equals average cost (AR = ATC) and now only

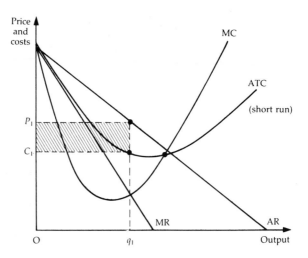

Figure 4.6 Monopolistic competition: short run

normal profit is earned. Only if a firm could either convince consumers that its product was superior – and hence worth paying more for – or obtain a cost advantage over rivals, would pure profits continue to be earned.

The monopolistic competition model suggests, therefore, that where there is a large number of suppliers with each supplying a similar product the following will occur:

- Competition will lower prices and profits as in a perfectly competitive market. However, the price will remain higher and the output lower than under perfect competition. The firm in a perfectly competitive market sets its price equal to marginal cost. In imperfect competition price is set above marginal cost. Since price reflects the consumer's marginal utility from the product and the marginal cost reflects the cost to society of providing it, where price exceeds marginal cost this implies a loss of welfare. This means that additional units could be supplied which would be worth more to consumers than it costs the firm to produce them.

- Production occurs at less than optimum scale. From Figure 4.7 it is clear that production, even in the long run, occurs at an output below that at which average cost is minimized (point X). Also, because a large number of firms are competing, economies of scale are unlikely.

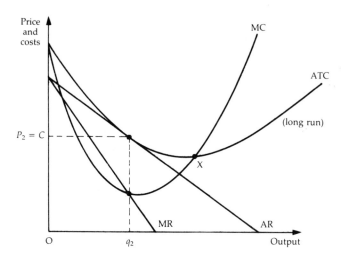

Figure 4.7 Monopolistic competition: long run

- Imperfect competition is associated with brand differentiation. This means more expenditure on advertising and packaging which raises costs. In so far as advertising is *informative*, it enables consumers to make better choices, though large-scale *competitive* advertising might be considered wasteful of society's scarce resources.

Oligopoly

Monopolistic competition requires a large number of competitors and free entry and exit. Many real-world markets today, however, are made up of a small number of suppliers and entry into and exit from the industry are restricted. Oligopoly is the term used to describe such markets. Where there are only two suppliers the term *duopoly* is used. Oligopolists may supply a relatively homogeneous product, such as oil, or they may compete through differentiated products, for example as in the motor car industry. The greater the product differentiation, the greater the scope to be a *price-maker* rather than a *price-taker*.

As there is a relatively small number of suppliers in the market, firms are interdependent and therefore competitive strategy must be based on some belief about the *reaction of rivals*, both in terms of price and non-price competition. How will competitors react to a price reduction, or a new advertising campaign, or extra investment, or development of a new product? If a firm introduces a new method of putting detergent into a washing machine by placing a liquid inside a plastic ball, how long will it take for the firm's competitors to respond? Could it limit the response by patenting the process? The substance of oligopolistic competition is that each firm's price and output decision is influenced by perceptions of rivals' countermoves.

Given the large number of possible reactions, several theories of oligopoly have been developed based on different assumptions about competitors' behaviour, the extent and form of entry and exit barriers, and the likelihood of collusion between suppliers. All have in common, however, the uncertainty which exists in oligopolistic markets regarding outcomes. The importance of rivals' reactions can be depicted as follows.

The oligopolist faces a downward sloping demand curve, but its nature is dependent on competitors' reactions to a price change, especially where products are similar. Suppose that currently the price charged by the oligopolist is P_1 and the firm is contemplating a price change to steal a competitive advantage and make more profit. Two demand curves are shown in Figure 4.8 depending on the response of the firm's competitors. Demand curve DD reflects the volumes that would be sold at different prices if competitors continued to sell at the same price. Demand curve dd shows the volumes that would be sold if competitors matched the price change. The demand curve DD is, of course, the more price elastic.

If the firm decided to reduce its price to P_2 to steal a competitive advantage, it would hope to travel down the curve DD (selling quantity q_3) and, with demand price elastic, increase its total earnings. However, if competitors responded by reducing their prices, demand would only rise to q_2, as shown by the demand curve dd. Lower prices might increase the market size, but there would be no switching of existing consumers away from competing supplies to the firm. For this reason we might expect total earnings to fall. Alternatively, our firm might raise its price hoping that other firms raise their prices too, leaving comparative prices unaffected. By charging more for each unit and total sales only marginally

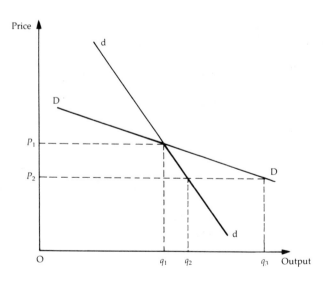

Figure 4.8 Oligopoly

reduced, total earnings rise. This is illustrated by a movement upwards along the demand curve dd. However, if competitors do not increase their prices there will be a movement up the DD curve and demand will plummet leading to a large fall in revenue.

A similar logic can be applied to changes in non-price competition, for example reactions to a new advertising campaign or the introduction of a new product. The possibilities can be summarized as follows:

- **Optimistic scenario.** This involves a movement up the demand curve dd following a price rise (rivals also raise their price therefore there is no competitive loss) and down the demand curve DD when price is reduced (rivals do not reduce their prices and therefore a competitive advantage is achieved).

- **Pessimistic scenario.** This is based upon a movement up the demand curve DD following a price rise (rivals fail to raise their prices leading to a competitive disadvantage) and down the demand curve dd when price is reduced (competitors also cut their prices). This produces, in effect, a 'kink' in the demand curve at the existing price (hence this analysis is often called by economists the 'kinked demand curve model').

The firm could attempt to place some probability weighting on the two scenarios. For example, based on past experience the firm might reckon that there is an 0.7 probability that its price reduction will spark off a similar reduction by competitors, i.e. it is 70% likely. Placing probabilities on rivals' reactions can also be applied to other competitive moves, for example how competitors might respond to a new advertising campaign, new investment, new product developments and so on. Of course, these probability weightings may in the event prove to be wrong (the past may be an unreliable guide to future reactions) and often they will be highly subjective.

Uncertainty about rivals' actions and reactions to competitive moves has led to the application by economists of the mathematical technique known as *game theory* to oligopolistic markets. Game theory attempts to identify the most profitable countermoves that could be made towards one's own 'best' strategy. On the basis of the answer, defensive measures are evolved.

A game occurs when there are two or more interacting decision-takers (*players*) and each decision or combination of decisions involves a particular outcome (*pay-off*). Applied to competition, it involves one firm choosing its optimal strategy on the basis that its competitors choose their optimal strategies. The general idea can be demonstrated through a simple example applied to a duopoly market.

The example deals with two firms, A and B, deciding new expenditures on promotion of their products. Figure 4.9 shows the *pay-off matrix*, i.e. the expected profit levels given high or low promotional expenditures. If both retain low expenditures on promotion, the expected profit for each is £20 million. If firm B opts for high spending but A retains low spending on promotion, B steals a competitive advantage and its profit rises to £34 million, while A's is expected to fall to £8 million. This is B's favoured outcome. However, equally, if firm A spends more on promotion but B does not, then it anticipates that its profit will rise to £30 million and B's will slump to £12 million. This is A's favoured outcome. However, A will expect that B will not allow it to gain in this way and hence will expect B to match its promotional expenditure. Therefore, the expected outcome is high promotional spending by *both firms* leading to profits of £16 million each. The problem with this outcome is that it produces lower profits than if both firms had not increased their spending on promotion.

In real-world markets the position will be more complex than our example. There are usually more than two suppliers and firms have to judge their competitors' actions and reactions not just for promotional spending but for all competitive activities. Nevertheless, the example does illustrate how oligopolistic outcomes can be *non-optimal* and why for the firms involved collusion is beneficial (in this case it would pay both firms to enter into a joint agreement not to increase promotional spending).

The existence of uncertainty about competitors' reactions can lead to a reluctance to change price or to be the first mover in non-price competition. Returning to our example in Figure 4.8, if the firm is uncertain which demand curve, DD or dd, will apply for any given price change, there may be an incentive not to alter price at all. Uncertainty about the likely response of competitors may produce a desire not to 'rock the boat' in markets.

We find in practice that the reaction of rivals to a price change (or to a change in any competitive variable) depends upon a host of factors. For example, firms may be more likely to match rivals' price cuts to preserve their market share when they already have excess capacity, e.g. the European car market in the 1991 recession. Also, the existence of economies of scale in an industry may increase the likelihood that competitors will respond to a price reduction by reducing their prices too or taking some other competitive reaction to limit the potential loss of sales. In such industries a loss of market

		FIRM B	
		Low	High
F I R M A	Low	(1) A = 20 B = 20	(2) A = 8 B = 34
	High	(3) A = 30 B = 12	(4) A = 16 B = 16

- Outcome (1) = Low promotional spending by both firms

- Outcome (2) = High promotional spending by firm B only

- Outcome (3) = High promotional spending by firm A only

Unstable since one firm can increase profits by spending more

- Outcome (4) = High promotional spending by both firms

Figure 4.9 Pay-off matrix for firms A and B with low and high promotional spending (£m)

share causes a significant rise in unit costs, further worsening competitiveness. By contrast, in industries with increasing costs firms may not be unhappy to reduce market share, perhaps as part of a longer-term strategy of withdrawal from the industry. Other factors which may impact on reactions to new competition are how profitable the market is to rivals, how fast it is growing (will one supplier's growth be at the expense of rivals?), and the stage in the trade cycle. Research suggests that in the post-war period prices have tended not to be sticky in many oligopolistic markets as predicted by the 'kinked demand curve' model, but inflation possibly explains this. Inflation makes consumers less resistant to rising prices.

We might also expect that when the industry is relatively new, there will be more uncertainty about rivals' reactions to both price and non-price competition and hence the age of the industry (or the stage in the product life cycle) may have a bearing on the nature of the competition in oligopolistic markets. Similarly, sudden shocks may provoke severe reactions in oligopolistic markets precisely because they do destroy existing settled positions. For example, deregulation of airline services in the United States led to frantic competition for passengers in the 1980s. Service levels were altered and prices slashed in a desperate attempt to remain competitive.

Within ten years of deregulation many new airlines (e.g. People Express) had failed and the major operators were merging in an attempt to cut losses and restore order in the market. Likewise, where new firms enter the market, especially with a new and superior product, or where a strong company outside the industry buys a company in the industry to launch new competition, this also delivers a major shock to complacent producers and often leads to major reactions in terms of price and non-price competition.

Therefore, not surprisingly, oligopolistic producers tend to take actions which prevent entry or at least deter it. The possibilities are many. For instance, existing suppliers may set prices equal to their average costs and if new producers face higher costs (because of start-up costs or a lack of economies of scale and scope) this limits new entry (a tactic known as *entry-limiting pricing*). They might even price below average cost, forgoing short-run profits with the objective of repelling potential rivals. They may also invest in additional capacity implying increased supply and hence lower prices and profits for new producers. Or non-price factors may be used to good advantage; for instance, brand proliferation by existing suppliers limits *space* in the market for new competitors' products (e.g. Unilever and Procter and Gamble in the detergents market). Alternatively, incumbent firms might undertake a major advertising campaign to preserve their market share.

Price leadership

In the 'kinked demand curve' analysis there was no *price leader*. In some oligopolistic markets uncertainty in the market is reduced because one supplier may decide to take the initiative and act as the *price leader*. When it alters its prices the competition follow suit. There are various possible types of price leadership in oligopolistic markets.

- **Dominant firm price leadership**. This exists when there is one large firm in the market and a number of smaller competitors. The dominant firm sets its own price, which the other firms then use as a guide for their prices. This works best where costs of production are similar, thus reducing the risk of any firm attempting to undercut the others' prices in a major way.
- **Collusive price leadership**. This exists where firms in an oligopolistic market collude on price. The collusion may be explicit or tacit.

- **Barometric price leadership**. In some markets one 'barometer' firm (it does not have to be the dominant firm) best assesses changes in demand and cost conditions and alters its price. The other firms then follow providing this is in their interests. The barometer firm may well change over time.

Competitive advantage

In a perfectly competitive market it is difficult to see what kind of competitive strategy a firm could adopt as products are homogeneous and each firm is a price-taker. But most real-world markets are well removed from being perfectly competitive. Even those markets which could come closest are often regulated. In almost all markets, therefore, there is scope to gain *competitive advantage*.

Much of the approach to competition in the economics literature has been based on the *structure–conduct–performance* paradigm (Figure 4.10). This is based on the idea that the structure of the market (namely the number of suppliers and their market shares) determines the conduct or behaviour of management, and that this in turn affects the performance of the industry in terms of prices and profits.

In recent years there has been some reaction to this approach because it does not allow for the effect of *potential* competition on the incumbent suppliers. It also implies that managerial conduct is simply a function of market structure. Research suggests that this is not the case. Firms facing similar levels of competition appear to exhibit different managerial behaviour and differing performance.

Nevertheless, the economists' market models do have important lessons for management interested in developing a competitive strategy. The main lessons are as follows:

- Whenever competition occurs in markets which are highly competitive and products cannot be differentiated in the eyes of consumers, e.g. by branding, then survival depends on keeping supply costs at least as low as competitors' costs. A firm must be the *lowest-cost producer* if it is to beat the competition. This follows since price is the only variable on which competition can centre. This leads to a search for cost savings through greater

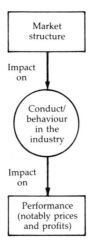

Figure 4.10   The structure–conduct–performance paradigm

output from existing resources and by investing in cost-saving processes. Firms which waste resources (i.e. are x-inefficient) will be unable to match competitors' prices and will be forced out of the market. Rivalry results in a search for lower costs, but it can also raise costs (e.g. promotion costs).

• In competitive markets, high profits tend to be competed away over time. Hence, leaving aside cost reduction, the only way to maintain high profits is to introduce new products and stay one step ahead of the competition. Therefore, surviving in a competitive market requires a high rate of technical innovation and new product development. The lowest-cost producer pricing at the market rate will make more profit than competitors, which can be ploughed back into the business.

• Where costs of production and products are identical (or closely so) there is limited scope to price to gain competitive advantage. Firms are price-takers, having to accept the going market price. One way for a supplier to break out of this constraint is to differentiate its product. The more the consumer perceives a product to be unique, the higher the price that can be charged and the less the threat from competitors. The differentiation strategy does have risks, however – the firm may be exposed in a market segment which is disappearing, e.g. the market for 'record players' in the face of new competition from compact discs. Whether to adopt a *broad* or a *narrow focus* is a critical strategic choice.

Once firms face differing demand conditions because of product differentiation and different cost structures (e.g. because of differing management ability) it is possible for some firms to continue to earn pure profit while others earn only normal profit. This explains why there tends to be a small range of prices in real-world competitive markets. Prices are closely clustered, rather than equal as predicted by the perfect competition model.

The existence of uncertainty about *if* and *how* competitors may react to a competitive move in an oligopolistic market suggests the following:

- Unless management believe their firm possesses some significant cost advantage over its competitors which will prevent them matching a price reduction, aggressive price cutting is a dangerous strategy. Reducing price may lead to a price war and ultimately financial disaster. Hence, it is often less risky (and perhaps less expensive) to compete through non-price variables such as promotion, new product development and achieving high quality. This helps to explain why, when demand falls, firms are reluctant to cut prices, even though a price reduction seems appropriate according to demand and supply analysis.

- Also, it usually takes much longer to develop a new rival product, invest in new capacity, orchestrate a rival promotion campaign and so on, than it does to change price. Therefore, firms can get a longer competitive lead by adopting non-price rather than price competition.

- A change in technology or new demand conditions may periodically produce a short period of price instability until a new market equilibrium is reached. Whenever there is a major 'shock' to the market, a period of raised uncertainty regarding competitors' moves can be expected.

- Uncertainty in oligopolistic markets can be reduced by collusion. For example, firms can agree in advance to raise prices together or to limit competitive advertising. By acting in concert, firms can turn a competitive market into, in effect, a monopolistic one. Collusion is often, therefore, an optimal strategy for producers, but, because it is usually at the expense of consumers, it tends to be illegal in most major countries (see Chapter 9).

There may, however, be fewer legislative barriers to merging with or taking over competitors – reducing the number of competitors can lower uncertainty in a market where collusion is prohibited. At the *international* level, a number of cartels exist to limit price competition in commodity markets. For example, the major world coffee producers have for many years operated an agreement on pricing to protect coffee-producing countries from the full effects of competition on earnings. A better known cartel is OPEC (the Organization of Petroleum Exporting Countries) which in the 1970s managed to restrict supplies and raise world oil prices dramatically. However, cartels tend not to flourish for long. The higher prices encourage a search for supplies from producers outside the cartel (e.g. the Alaskan and North Sea oil fields). Also, cartels are prone to production-quota busting by cartel members keen to cash in on the higher prices.

Generic strategies for competitive advantage

The Harvard academic, Michael Porter (Porter, 1985), has crystallized from the market models explored in this chapter what he calls two generic strategies for gaining competitive advantage:

- **Lowest-cost producer**. A firm can aim to be the *lowest-cost producer*, thereby underpricing the competition. It is important, however, that the consumer does not perceive the products to be 'cheap and nasty'. Also, firms competing solely on price remain exposed to even lower-cost producers and rivals who entice consumers away with higher quality substitutes.

- **Product differentiation**. A firm can develop *differentiated products* (through innovation and marketing) and charge premium prices. This can lead in turn to a 'focus' strategy, i.e. focusing on particular narrow or broad product areas or markets.

According to Porter, failure in competitive markets is associated with being 'stuck in the middle'. In Figure 4.11 firm A, despite an undifferentiated product, has competitive advantage because of low production costs, while firm B also has competitive advantage despite high production costs because of product differentiation. Firm C, however, is 'stuck in the middle'. A firm which is neither the lowest-cost producer nor the producer of differentiated products lacks competitive advantage. Study of a number of markets suggests

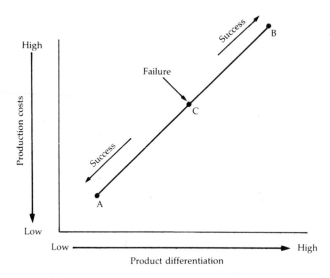

Figure 4.11 A representation of Porter's generic strategies for gaining competitive advantage

that this analysis is reasonably robust though some economists object to the idea that these are either/or strategies. Japanese manufacturers have gained competitive advantage *both* by raising the quality of their goods and at the same time by driving down their costs of production. Even the most highly differentiated producer should keep an eye on costs which do not add value to the consumer.

Competitive advantage of nations

Most recently Porter has extended his analysis to an explanation of the competitive advantage of nations. He asks why some countries have performed well since the war (notably Japan), sweeping the competition aside, while others appear to have lost out in world markets (notably the United Kingdom and the United States). Porter argues that four broad attributes of a nation determine success. These are illustrated in Figure 4.12 (the figure is often referred to as Porter's 'diamond'). This 'diamond' shapes the environment faced by firms and either promotes or impedes the creation of competitive advantage. The four attributes are as follows:

1. The quantity and quality of factors of production (e.g. skilled labour force and infrastructure).

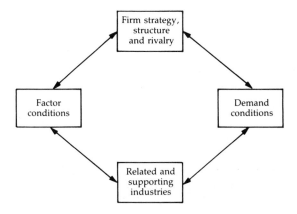

Figure 4.12 Porter's 'diamond' (Source: M. Porter (1990), *The Competitive Advantage of Nations*, London: Macmillan)

2. The nature of the demand for products (especially a demand for high-quality goods).
3. The existence of related and supporting industries which are internationally competitive.
4. Firm strategy, structure and rivalry.

While all four attributes are important, the latter is of most interest here. Porter's central message is that tough domestic rivalry breeds international success. Although the current fashion is to talk about firms operating 'globally', this does not rule out domestic competition. Indeed, Porter argues that Japan's success in international markets lies in having not one dominant supplier in an industry but numerous competing suppliers. There are nine car manufacturers, fifteen TV manufacturers, twenty-five suppliers of audio equipment and fifteen camera producers in Japan. By contrast, Japan's cartelized industries, like those in the United States, Germany and Switzerland are relatively uncompetitive. Porter argues that the force of domestic competition and the battle to survive in the home market generates the search for high-quality products at low cost. Competition is the spur in Japan and elsewhere for rapid technological change.

In certain circumstances competitors may gain through joint R&D projects and in some industries only one domestic supplier may be able to operate close to minimum efficient scale (e.g. aircraft manufacture). Therefore, Porter's analysis does not rule out mergers and joint ventures altogether. It does, however, serve as an important reminder of the importance of competition to national survival and counsels against hasty mergers aimed at defending the domestic market. The central message of Porter's analysis is that in the future, as import barriers are dismantled, the successful domestic producer will be one that is also successful on the world stage.

Concluding remarks

In this chapter we have been concerned with how the competitive environment impacts on businesses. Four main market models – perfect competition, monopoly, monopolistic competition and oligopoly – have featured, designed as tools of analysis which managers can use when analyzing the competitive environment in which they operate. Once the nature of the competitive environment in which the business operates is determined, an appropriate competitive strategy can be formulated so as to win over the customer. This strategy will be based on a 'competitive analysis', which will involve a consideration of customer demands, product developments, the firm's strengths and weaknesses, and the strengths and weaknesses of competitors alongside their likely response to any competitive move. Ultimately, as we have seen, two broad strategies usually exist – competing on price (cost) or non-price factors – though they are not necessarily mutually exclusive. Since industries go through life cycles and product markets change, it is important to appreciate that what is the most appropriate strategy in one period may not be the best for another. For example, in the early years there may be many new entrants and an expanding market, so price is not so important. At the maturity stage of the industry cycle, as market growth slows down, price competition may become more intense and firms which can clearly differentiate their products steal an advantage. Finally, when the market begins to decline only the most cost efficient or highly differentiated firms might survive.

The precise competitive strategy adopted by the firm has implications for pricing policy, as we shall see in Chapter 6, but first we turn to the important issue of managerial objectives.

5

Managerial objectives and the firm

The essence of managerial objectives

In the previous chapter we assumed that the firm's primary objective is to maximize profit. This assumption underlies the competitive environment which we mapped out using the frameworks of the perfect competition, monopoly, monopolistic competition and oligopoly market models, and which allowed us to establish benchmarks for the analysis and comparison of price–output decisions under different market structures. This approach, often referred to as the traditional (or 'neoclassical') approach, can readily be criticized, however, on the grounds that it does not provide a satisfactory explanation of real-world production and pricing decisions. By assuming away many complexities, the simplistic assumption of profit maximization enables us to make very clear-cut predictions about the firm's behaviour. However, it is one thing to make predictions, but another to say how realistic they are or how accurate they are. The traditional theory of the firm seems to be at its best when analyzing behaviour in perfectly competitive and monopoly market structures. In practice, however, these theoretical extremes are rarely to be found – in reality most firms are confronted with market conditions which are more readily described as imperfectly competitive with oligopoly being the dominant market form. This is not to say that we should dismiss the analysis presented in the previous chapter – on the contrary, it is essential to the development of a deeper understanding of the fundamental relationships between pricing and production decisions.

Most economists sympathize with the defence of the profit maximization assumption, recognizing its usefulness as a mental, theoretical link to explaining how one gets from the 'cause to the effect'. The models reviewed in the last chapter were developed to *predict*, not describe, behaviour in markets. Since the 1950s, however, a collection of new, alternative theories of corporate behaviour have been put forward. The purpose of this chapter is to review these theories and to assess their merits in terms of realism alongside the traditional approach. We shall consider these new theories under the following three basic headings:

- Agency theory.
- Managerial theories.
- Behavioural theories.

A fourth area of development has already been discussed in Chapter 4 in the study of oligopoly. There we introduced the concept of 'game theory' which represents a major development in understanding real-world corporate behaviour.

The new theories which we shall discuss below stem, in the main, from abandoning one or both of the following assumptions which are central to the traditional approach, namely that:

- decisions are made under conditions of perfect knowledge, and
- the objective of the firm is to maximize profits.

There are four main reasons which can be offered as justification for abandoning these two assumptions. These relate to the following:

- The growth in oligopoly.
- The growth of managerial capitalism.
- Difficulties surrounding profit maximization in practice.
- The organizational complexity of firms.

Before examining the alternative theories of corporate behaviour listed above we shall briefly discuss the significance of each of these developments in turn.

The growth in oligopoly

As mentioned above, oligopoly is the most common form of market structure in reality and yet it is the structure to which the traditional assumptions fit least well. Empirical evidence of the growing importance of oligopoly can be found by measuring the degree of concentration across industries using one of the methods outlined in the previous chapter. When an industry is concentrated, but not a monopoly, it displays the characteristics of oligopoly. Empirical studies of a number of countries have shown a general trend across many industries towards this type of market structure throughout the last century.

There are two reasons why the traditional theory of the firm, based on the assumptions of perfect knowledge and profit-maximizing behaviour, fails to provide a satisfactory explanation of market behaviour under oligopoly. These concern:

(a)   the extent to which firms are interdependent, and

(b)   the degree of uncertainty that exists in oligopolistic markets.

These issues have already been fully discussed in Chapter 4. Briefly, mutual interdependence arises in oligopoly because each firm produces a sufficiently large proportion of the industry's total output for its behaviour to affect the market share of its competitors. Uncertainty arises because the behaviour of one firm is conditioned not just by what its rivals are doing but also by what it thinks its rivals *might* do in response to any initiative of its own. Uncertainty and interdependence are best tackled through a game theory approach to market behaviour.

The growth of managerial capitalism

The traditional assumption of profit maximization implies that the 'firm' somehow has a mind of its own, capable of arriving at independent, rational decisions. In reality, of course, firms do not make any decisions – it is entrepreneurs and managers (i.e. individuals) who make business decisions. A 'firm' is nothing more than an abstract concept covering owners, managers and employees.

Over time, the relationship between *ownership* and *control* in firms has changed substantially. In their earliest form business units or firms were owned and managed by the same people, therefore the assumption of profit maximization did not seem unreasonable. Over time, however, with the growth of large corporations and the dominance of public joint-stock companies, there has emerged a separation of ownership from control. Ownership is in the hands of shareholders who may or may not exercise their voting rights at board meetings. Control, however, is largely in the hands of the managers and directors of the firm. This situation is described as *managerial capitalism* and has given rise to 'managerial theories' to explain the behaviour of firms (see later). With managers in control it is easy to question the validity of the profit maximization assumption of the traditional theory. Some managers may seek to keep shareholders happy by reporting a certain level of profit while leaving themselves the flexibility to achieve, perhaps personal, objectives (such as business growth, diversification, salary, etc.). Even if profit maximization is stated as the key objective of the firm as a whole, it is unlikely that every individual within the firm, even within senior management, will be pursuing this objective consistently.

There appears, therefore, to be a potential division between the goal of shareholders and the goal of management in the real world. Recently this issue has been approached through *agency theory* (see pages 104–6).

Difficulties surrounding profit maximization

In practice, businesses may have insufficient accurate information about demand and cost conditions to be able to use the concepts of marginal revenue and marginal cost as the basis for determining the profit-maximizing output. Pricing policies in practice are often determined by other methods, such as on the basis of a mark-up over average unit costs subject to the achievement of a 'required' profit margin. As much of the output as possible will then be sold on the market at this price.

Other price guidelines may be followed for different firms in different industries. For example, over the years two basic pricing guidelines for state industries have emerged: *marginal-cost pricing*, and *mark-up pricing* to achieve a target rate of return. Full details of these and other pricing policies are given in Chapter 6. The key point to note here, however, is that the traditional theory of the firm does not provide a particularly useful framework for analyzing the behaviour of state firms.

The organizational complexity of firms

A final reason for questioning the validity of the traditional approach to understanding the behaviour of firms relates to the changing organizational structure of firms. As with the growth of managerial capitalism, this reflects the fact that as firms have increased in size, so too they have become much more complex in terms of their organizational structure. This structure will reflect the often conflicting views of owners, managers, workers and consumers. Within each grouping there will be still more complex structures: perhaps different categories of shareholders with different share holdings who are interested in different objectives (short-term versus long-term profits perhaps); different managers at different levels with different aims and aspirations; blue-collar workers and white-collar workers with different career expectations and reward packages, perhaps represented by different unions; finally, there will be different groups of consumers to be satisfied (such as the one-off customer versus the long-term, loyal customer).

Given the degree of complexity of organizational structures today, some economists argue that it is unlikely that a useful theory of business decisions can be based on a *single* objective and that instead the subject should be approached through a study of the behaviour of individuals or groups within the firm. Also, it is held that such an approach should start from the position that people in firms, including managers, do not aim to maximize anything – they simply aim to 'satisfy' a range of objectives. This 'behavioural' approach to the firm will be discussed later in the chapter.

In summary, therefore, the traditional theory of profit maximization as illustrated in Chapter 4 may be criticized because:

- it is not readily applicable to oligopoly situations;
- it is no longer appropriate in today's environment, where managerial capitalism has taken over from entrepreneurial capitalism and where control has become divorced from ownership;
- pricing policies in practice may bear little obvious resemblance to those suggested by the MR = MC principle, and
- the complexity of organizational structures today calls into question some of the basic assumptions of the traditional theory.

We turn now to discuss some developments that have taken place in the analysis of the behaviour of firms, starting with the concept of *agency theory* referred to already. This theory recognizes the growth in managerial capitalism and the complexity of modern organizational structures.

Agency theory

The broad thrust of agency theory as a basis for understanding the behaviour of firms is summarized in Figure 5.1 below which shows the *agent–principal* relationships that exist in the private and public sectors. In the private sector, the *principals* are those who ultimately have the rights to the assets or who 'own' the firm. In joint-stock companies these are the shareholders and they appoint directors as *agents* to manage these assets on their behalf. In theory, the directors should manage the assets in the interests of the principals but in practice this cannot be guaranteed. In practice, therefore, the agent–principal relationship may involve costs in terms of lower efficiency. This is likely to mean that the principals face costs, not

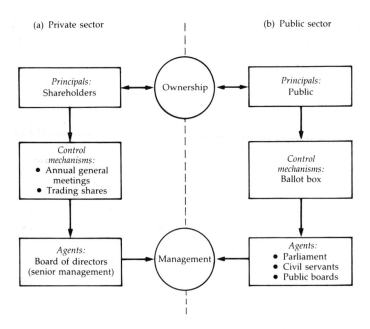

Figure 5.1 The agent–principal relationship: private v. public sector

least in terms of the time and effort involved in monitoring the work of their agents.

There is, however, a 'control mechanism' in the *private* sector. Shareholders may attend company annual general meetings to question and, if necessary, replace the directors. Perhaps more importantly, the shareholders can exercise their right to sell their share holdings altogether. Many economists argue that the existence of such a control mechanism acts as a major constraint on private sector management. If management pursues a quiet life or other objectives which reduce profitability, then shareholders can react by disposing of their shares. This will tend to drive down the share price, making the company vulnerable to a takeover by new management.

On the other hand, some economists question the significance of shareholder power, arguing instead that shareholders are fairly inert to management performance. Most shareholders rarely attend annual general meetings and the existence of transactions costs and capital gains taxation may reinforce a tendency to hold onto shares in the hope that things will get better. If things do get better those who have held on to their shares benefit and this produces a 'free rider' problem. Shareholders may be reluctant to sell, hoping, however, other shareholders do sell. Further, it is not obvious that it is necessarily the less profitable firms which succumb to a takeover. Sometimes what appear to be profitable, well-managed firms face hostile takeover bids.

Figure 5.1 also illustrates the agent–principal relationship which exists in the *public* sector. In this case, civil servants and public boards manage industries and services on behalf of the public. Since there are no shares to sell or annual general meetings to attend, the public are unable to indicate directly dissatisfaction with management performance. Voters can express their views on government performance through the ballot box, but this is a crude indicator of satisfaction and dissatisfaction with particular state activities (such as the postal service, police, education, etc.). Votes reflect broad manifesto pledges and not, usually, views about the quality of service from one particular public industry or state sector. For this reason there appears to be greater scope for managerial discretionary behaviour by management in the public sector compared with the private sector. Consequently, there may be a tendency for production costs in the public sector to be higher than in the private sector – an important rationale for the worldwide privatization programme of the 1980s.

A further constraint on managerial discretionary behaviour relates to the *product market*. Firms, whether private or public sector (unless backed by considerable taxpayers' funds), must be efficient to survive in competitive markets. Any inefficiency which leads to higher prices will be penalized through a loss of market share and eventual bankruptcy. This constraint is illustrated in Figure 5.2 below, which shows the long-run equilibrium of the firm in a perfectly competitive market (for a full explanation of the diagram see page 75). In the long run only normal profits are earned by the firm. If AC_1 represents the average cost curve for efficient firms in the industry and AC_2 the curve for the less efficient ones, then the latter firms will make losses and go out of business. As a general rule we can conclude, therefore, that non-profit goals which raise costs are likely to be more prevalent in firms operating where product market competition is imperfect (since if the market was perfectly competitive the firm would not be able to afford the luxury of non-profit goals).

Managerial theories

Once we acknowledge that managers in the private and perhaps more especially in the public sector are able, to some degree, to pursue their own goals rather than that of profit maximization, the question arises as to what are these goals and what is the effect on prices and outputs. We shall consider the following three possible goals:

- **Sales revenue maximization.**
- **Managerial utility maximization.**
- **Corporate growth maximization.**

The common feature of the underlying models concerned with these goals is that they each reject the simple profit maximization assumption, replacing it with an alternative target which management aims to achieve. These targets stem from the study of what motivates different managers where there is a separation of ownership from the management (control) function, i.e. an agency relationship, which leaves managers with some degree of freedom to pursue non-profit goals, at least in the short term.

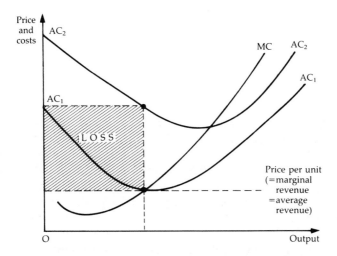

Figure 5.2 The importance of the product market

Sales revenue maximization

The idea of sales revenue maximization as a management goal was first put forward by Professor William Baumol in 1959. The argument is based on Baumol's own research into managerial behaviour and is couched in terms of oligopolistic industry, in which there is a divorce of ownership and management of resources. Baumol argues that managers are likely to attach a great importance to achieving high sales revenues for the following reasons:

1. High and expanding sales revenues help to attract external finance to the firm – larger firms generally find it easier to raise capital, while financial institutions may be less willing to deal with a firm suffering from declining sales.
2. High sales assist the distribution and retailing of products – resulting in economies from selling in bulk.
3. Consumers may view a firm with falling sales in a less favourable light – this may deter consumers from buying and reduce sales even further.
4. The distributive trade may be less co-operative, for example to extend credit lines, when a firm's sales are declining.
5. Falling sales may result in reductions in staffing levels, including managerial staff, as costs are cut.

6. Last, but not least, managers' salaries may well depend on fast growth of sales revenues – managers are rewarded for expanding business.

Baumol's theory does not ignore profit altogether but is presented in terms of sales revenue maximization subject to a *minimum profit constraint* on the firm. As long as this constraint is met, based on the assumption that this will be sufficient to pacify shareholders, the firm will aim to maximize sales revenues. The needs of shareholders cannot be ignored but the minimum profit constraint will usually be less than the maximum profit feasible. Presumably this will especially hold true where shareholders do not know what is the maximum profit that could conceivably be achieved. Lack of information on the part of shareholders may lead them to accept the reported profit. We might expect this to be most prevalent where there are no competitor firms reporting profits to facilitate comparisons.

Figure 5.3 illustrates the principles of the sales revenue maximization model where the total revenue (TR) and total cost (TC) curves are drawn for a typical firm. The curve ef shows the total profit or loss and is derived from the TR and TC curves for each level of sales. It will be seen that the output which maximizes profit is q_3, i.e. where the vertical distance between TR and TC is at its greatest. At outputs q_1 and q_6 TR = TC and therefore profit is zero. To the left of q_1 and to the right of q_6, TR is less than TC and therefore losses are being made.

In the absence of a minimum profit constraint, management could pursue sales revenues by expanding output up to q_5 where TR is at its maximum (the firm would not wish to increase output beyond this point because total revenue would fall). With the imposition of a minimum profit constraint, such as a level X as shown in Figure 5.3, sales can now only be expanded up to q_4. Expansion beyond this point would lead to a reduction in total profits below the minimum level considered acceptable to shareholders (note that the profit constraint is also met at output q_2 but since output q_4 provides a higher level of sales revenue, a sales revenue-maximizing management would not choose q_2 over q_4).

With the pursuit of sales revenue constrained by the required profit level, any increase in this level (shifting the profit constraint line at X upwards) would lead to a reduction in output, whereas any reduction in the required profit would lead to an expansion in output. Note that only if the profit constraint line passes through point A would production be at the level to maximize profits. From this model we can conclude that, in contrast to management which

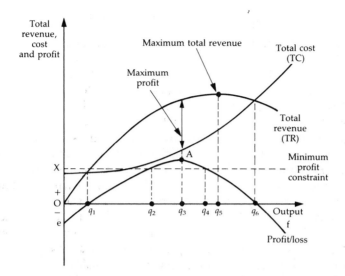

Figure 5.3 Sales revenue maximization

attempts to profit-maximize, a sales revenue-maximizing management will tend to:

- Produce at a higher output level.
- Set prices lower (since given a normal downward sloping demand curve a higher output can only be sold at a lower price).
- Invest more heavily in measures that boost demand, such as advertising (to increase demand without reducing price).

In later formulations of his model Professor Baumol substituted as the objective of management the maximization of the *growth* of the firm for the maximization of sales revenue. The two goals are, of course, related, though growth maximization is a more dynamic concept. Also, whereas in the sales revenue maximization model the profit constraint could be at any level (whatever keeps the shareholders happy), in the growth model it is set by the 'means for obtaining capital needed to finance expansion plans', i.e. by the need to attract finance for investment. The 'optimal profit stream' is that which is consistent with raising adequate investment funds to achieve the highest rate of growth of output *over the firm's lifetime*.

Managerial utility maximization

Baumol's model outlined above implies that management has some choice in the trade-off between profit and sales revenue in business decision-making. This recognition has led to the development of other models which explain firms' behaviour in terms of *managerial discretion*. One important approach was developed by the American economist Oliver Williamson in the 1960s. He argued that managers in large firms have enough discretion to pursue those policies which give them personally most satisfaction. Whereas shareholders are assumed to equate their level of satisfaction (i.e. 'utility') with profit, management is considered to have utility functions which include a number of personal goals and personal measures of 'well-being'. These goals may include the achievement of a plush office, a large company car, a high salary, etc. In fact, the goal of sales revenue maximization could even be interpreted as a special case where that single goal dominates all other managerial goals or is even the means by which the other managerial goals are realized.

Williamson's model makes allowance for markets not being perfectly competitive and for the agent–principal relationship in firms described by Figure 5.1. He suggests that managers' self-interest could be seen in terms of the achievement of goals in four particular areas, namely:

- **High salaries**. This includes not just take-home pay but also all other forms of monetary income such as bonuses and share options. The desire for large salaries reflects a desire for a high standard of living, and a high status.
- **Staff under their control**. This refers to both the number and quality of subordinate staff as a measure of status and a measure of power (reflecting the 'I hire them, I fire them' type of management philosophy).
- **Discretionary investment expenditure**. This does not refer to investment that is essential for the success of the firm but rather to any investment over and above this amount. This includes any pet projects of the management that are excused as necessary to the general development of the firm (such as sponsorship, say, of Formula One motor racing in the case of a petrol company). The manager may be able to further his or her own personal interests and hobbies (sponsoring staff golf outings, for example). The extent of the manager's authority over discretionary expenditure may be taken as an indication of his or her status.

- **Fringe benefits**. Managers might strive for an expense account, a lavishly furnished office, a company car, free club memberships, etc. These perks may be part of the 'slack' in the organization – i.e. non-essential expenditures that force up the firm's costs.

Williamson expresses these goals in terms of a *utility function*. Believing that the first two goals (concerning salaries and staff) are closely related, he combines them under the symbol S. Discretionary investment is represented by I_d while M represents expenditure on managerial perks. Using U to denote utility which the manager seeks to maximize, Williamson presents the following managerial utility function:

$$U = f(S, I_d, M)$$

Profits are not ignored by Williamson. Like Baumol, he recognizes that a minimum profit must be paid to shareholders but argues that managers will strive to increase their utility as long as this profit constraint is being satisfied. Equally, however, it is possible to conceive of management desiring higher profits because they derive satisfaction from business achievement. Profitability is a measure of business success and buoyant profits provide a fertile environment in which managers can then pursue other goals.

Corporate growth maximization

The third and final variation of the managerial theory of firms' behaviour which we present here also sees managerial motivation in terms of striving to maximize a target. This time the target is growth. The model is associated with the work of the Cambridge economist Professor Robin Marris in the 1960s. Again, competition is assumed to be limited, with ownership divorced from management so that there is scope for managerial discretionary behaviour. The theory stems from Marris's view of the institutional framework and organization of the modern corporation. He sees the firm as typically a bureaucratic organization – a self-perpetuating structure where corporate growth and the security that it brings is seen as a desirable end in itself. Managers are expected to see a relationship between the growth of the company and hence profits ploughed back into investment, and their own personal goals (such as increased status, power and salary). At the same time, managers are expected to balance growth against the impact on profits and dividends – they must beware of the danger of low dividends depressing share prices which may leave the firm vulnerable to a hostile takeover bid. Therefore, growth and security compete as objectives and each requires a different approach to risk in terms of investment and capital raising.

In particular, there may be a trade-off between securing profits to pay dividends and taking risks when investing to increase the growth of the firm. At the same time, while profits provide the retained earnings to help finance new investment which leads to growth, excessive company liquidity may attract predators. Cash-rich companies attract takeover bids. In Marris's model this conflict is summarized as management seeking the *optimal dividend-to-profit retention ratio*.

Behavioural theories

The approaches to managerial goals considered so far go well beyond the simple notion of profit maximization. However, they still cling to the idea that management does endeavour to maximize *something*, whether it be sales revenue, utility or growth, although in a world of uncertainty and large organizations it could be argued that maximizing behaviour of any kind is not relevant. A radically different approach which is adopted by so-called 'behaviouralists' rejects the whole notion of maximization in favour of a less strong goal of 'satisficing'. Whereas the traditional profit-maximizing model and the alternatives reviewed so far in this chapter have been concerned with how firms *should* behave to maximize profits, sales revenue, etc., the behaviouralist approach is concerned with how firms *actually* behave with attention focused on the internal decision-making structure of the firm. The aim is to understand this decision-making process rather than to try and make predictions about price and output.

The idea of 'satisficing' was initially introduced by Professor H. A. Simon in the 1950s. He argued that, faced with incomplete information and uncertainty, individuals are more likely to be content to achieve a *satisfactory* level of something rather than to strive to *maximize* goals, and that this level will be revised continuously in the light of experience. This notion was further developed by R. M. Cyert and J. G. March who established a behaviouralist model of the firm. As noted above, the *process* of decision-making, ignored in the other models of the firm discussed earlier, is of critical importance. According to Cyert and March, the firm can be thought of as a *coalition* of various interest groups: different departments, different levels of management, different groups of workers, suppliers and consumers, shareholders, etc. Hence, a complex process of bargaining must take place between these various groups within the firm to determine their *collective* goals. Some of the goals could be related to the following:

- **Production:** a goal that output must lie within a certain satisfactory range.
- **Sales:** a goal that there must be a satisfactory level of sales.
- **Market share**: a goal indicating a satisfactory size of market share as a measure of comparative success as well as growth.
- **Profit**: still an important goal, but one amongst many rather than necessarily of overriding importance.

Consequently, there is no single objective of the firm; instead, there are multiple goals which emerge from the potential for conflict amongst interest groups within the firm. In addition, these goals can be expected to alter over time as circumstances change. Different managers from different departments or sections of the organization will have a strong affiliation for targets in their own areas. For example, sales personnel will tend to identify with the goals of marketing and sales departments, while the accountants will tend to identify with financial outcomes and the interests of the finance department. There is no necessity that the goals of these different groups should be the same or easily reconcilable. In these circumstances the objectives of the firm are eventually determined by factors such as the following:

- Bargaining between groups and the relationship between groups within the firm.
- The method by which objectives are formulated within the organization.
- How groups and, therefore, the 'firm' react to experiences and make adjustments.

Hence, the various goals set by different departments within the organization may well conflict and it may arise that managers will be prepared to sacrifice some profit to achieve other goals. The way in which such conflicts are resolved draws attention to *the process* of decision-making within organizations.

The goals may be inconsistent but it is possible to see how they can be reconciled if we introduce the idea of *satisficing* in the place of maximizing behaviour. The aim will be to achieve a satisfactory performance for each of the goals. For example, sales staff might accept what they regard as a 'satisfactory' level of sales growth to maintain an agreed profitability, while finance staff agree to the firm forgoing some immediate profit by raising spending on advertising. With such compromises within the organization, Cyert and March argue that different groupings can be bought off by 'side payments' when their particular goals are not being met. These side payments can take pecuniary or non-pecuniary forms, such as higher pay for a section of staff or plusher offices for production managers. Similarly, disgruntled shareholders might be bought off by a rise in dividends per share. Naturally, there may be groups who are able to exert a greater influence on objectives from time to time. Psychology plays a key role in the management of the firm in the way just described since people's actions are to a degree a result of their aspirations, which in turn stem from their perception of how well they feel they ought to be doing within the firm.

In summary, the essence of the behaviouralist approach lies in the study of human beings in terms of their relationship with their environment. Within the complex environment of the firm, be-haviour can be seen as a compromise between conflicting views and interests. In achieving a compromise so that the firm can function it is unlikely that any one goal could ever be maximized, at least for long.

Concluding remarks

The behaviouralist approach to the firm has won many adherents because it appears to be the most descriptively realistic. Rather than simply *assuming* some maximization objective (profits, sales, etc.), it seeks to explore the internal decision-making of the firm and the process by which the goals emerge. It allows for and copes with conflicting and changing goals which the other theories reviewed in this chapter avoid. Also, it is concerned with *how* firms reach decisions and *why*. Its main weakness, however, lies in its lack of generality and thus predictive ability. Clearly, maximization of something is easier to model than satisficing behaviour. Since every firm is different, we may need a different 'behavioural theory' for each firm. In truth, economists prefer economic models which are generally applicable and which have predictive ability even when this is gained at the expense of descriptive reality.

The other approaches to the firm discussed in this chapter provide interesting variations on the traditional profit-maximizing assumption. In the sense that they highlight managerial discretionary behaviour, the choice of goals, goal conflict and the constraints upon management decisions, they have considerable value. However, as with the behavioural theory, most economists regard them as supplements to the profit-maximizing model, at least in relation to the private sector; in the public sector where there is often no profit goal they are clearly appropriate.

The profit-maximizing model, set out in Chapter 4, still prevails. Even within the alternative models put forward, profit exists as an important constraint upon management and it is still the case that the profit-maximizing model serves us well in predicting how price and output will change when, for example, product taxes are raised, costs of production increase or market price is lowered. Moreover, some economists stress that profit maximization and the other models of the firm can be reconciled through a more careful definition of profit maximization which stipulates the *time period* concerned. Sales revenue growth, for example, may be the target set to achieve a greater market share with a view to making larger profits in the longer term.

The importance of the different theories reviewed in this chapter arises from the insight they provide into the impact of different managerial objectives on the behaviour of firms and, more specifically, price and output decisions. Determination of the firm's goal or goals is a crucial first step in developing an effective competitive strategy. Only once we clearly define where we want to go can we begin to decide how to get there. The next chapter focuses on the different pricing policies which can be adopted. The precise policy chosen will, of course, amongst other things, reflect management's precise objectives.

6

Understanding pricing strategies

The essence of pricing strategies

Choosing the appropriate price to charge for a good or service is one of the most important challenges facing management. Set the price too low and the result will be overwhelming demand and frustrated customers, much as existed in Eastern bloc countries where governments kept prices low for social and political reasons in the post-war period. Set the price too high and there will be stockpiles of unsold goods and a probable cash flow crisis. Determining the right price to sell all of the production profitably and at the same time to leave no unsatisfied customers, that is to say customers who wanted to buy at that price, is like trying to balance a set of kitchen scales – too much weight on either side will cause the scales to tilt. Not surprisingly, therefore, economists call the price which exactly matches the supply and demand for a particular good or service, the *equilibrium price*.

This chapter considers the various approaches to pricing that managers might adopt. In particular, we examine the following topics:

- Price determination and managerial objectives.
- Generic pricing strategies.
- Pricing and the competitive environment.
- The marketing mix and the product life cycle.

- The economics of price discrimination.
- Pricing in multi-plant and multi-product firms.
- Peak-load pricing.
- Pricing policy and the role of government.

In practice, the 'best' or 'correct' price to charge must remain uncertain ahead of actual production and sale. Market conditions are in a constant state of flux which produces uncertainty and therefore pricing decisions contain no small element of risk. However, so that the basic techniques of optimal pricing strategies can be fully analyzed, the assumption is often made in this chapter that pricing decisions are being made with full or perfect information available to managers about consumer demand, competitors' reactions, supply costs, etc. This is highly unrealistic but it provides a useful starting point for the formulation of best-practice pricing.

Price determination and managerial objectives

Price serves two broad functions. All managers will be familiar with the first of these – *prices raise revenue for the firm*. Price multiplied by the quantity sold determines the firm's total revenue and, depending on production costs, ultimately the firm's survival. But the second broad function is of equal importance in that *price is a rationing device*. It rations out the available production amongst consumers on the basis of their ability and willingness to pay. Chapter 2 contained a detailed discussion of consumer demand in which the importance of the demand relationship and of price elasticity were emphasized. At any given time consumers are likely to buy more of a good or service only if its price is reduced (assuming the other conditions of demand such as income and tastes stay unchanged). In stating this, it is not essential to view consumers as always logical and rational, as always achieving maximum satisfaction from their limited income. Economists do not believe that consumers are professional accountants always carrying a portable computer when going about their shopping! All that is essential is that consumers, in general, *respond* to prices. Not surprisingly, this appears to be borne out in reality. Later in the chapter we will also consider other factors than price that may influence buying decisions, in a discussion of the 'marketing mix'.

Since price is an important determinant of the amount sold, it follows that it also determines the amount supplied. When price is reduced and demand rises, the firm will attempt to cash in by increasing supply. In turn this means that investment projects are directly dependent on the expected prices of the product concerned. In deciding whether to invest, some judgement must be made regarding likely prices over the lifetime of the investment project (or at least over the period in which cash flows are being discounted to present values – see Chapter 7). Once the decision has been taken to produce and the investment has been installed, pricing is more tightly constrained. Hence, the greatest freedom in choosing a pricing strategy comes at the planning stage. It must, therefore, be an integral part of investment planning. In general terms, the higher the expected price the bigger the output the firm will want to supply and hence the larger will be the investment in capacity that the firm will be willing to make. Just as demand is a function of price, so too is supply, as we saw earlier in Chapter 3.

Price determination

In a competitive market economy price is determined by the forces of demand and supply. A good example is the market for colour TVs, where there are a number of suppliers – Sony, Hitachi, National Panasonic, Philips, Ferguson, etc. – each attempting to sell to consumers. The consumer may, of course, not buy on the basis of price alone (though no doubt many do), but for the present we shall concentrate on price as the principal determinant. Figure 6.1 illustrates the general market situation for one of these suppliers, e.g. Sony. The demand curve for Sony TVs is downward sloping, implying that more sets will be sold as the retail price is reduced. The demand curve has also been drawn to suggest that the demand for Sony TVs is price elastic (price sensitive) around price P_1. In practice, Sony's marketing will be aimed at creating 'brand loyalty', but we shall assume that many consumers will still switch to competitors' products if the relative price of a Sony TV is increased. Therefore, when Sony raises its prices, say from P_1 to P_2, and competitors' prices are unaltered, the expectation is that the demand for Sony TVs will fall from q_1 to q_2. Equally, if Sony reduces the price of its sets, say from P_1 to P_3, and its competitors do not follow suit, the demand will rise from q_1 to q_3.

The supply curve in Figure 6.1 shows how many TVs Sony will be willing to supply at each price and reflects the marginal costs of producing TV sets (for an explanation of this point see Chapter 3).

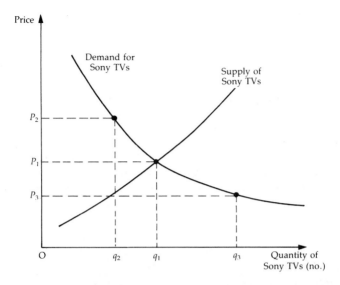

Figure 6.1 The market for Sony TVs

Provided that price is set at P_1 the market will be cleared – hence P_1 is the equilibrium price. All consumers wanting to buy Sony TVs at that price are able to obtain them and Sony is left with no unsatisfied demand or unsold stocks. Clearly, if the price is established above P_1, Sony will want to sell more TV sets as it is now more profitable to do so, but consumers will be less willing to buy them. The result is unsold sets (i.e. stocks). Equally, if Sony reduces the price below P_1, demand will expand, but given that supplying is now less profitable, output will contract, leaving unsatisfied customers.

In practice, the conditions of demand, such as consumer perceptions of the product or competitors' prices, and the conditions of supply, notably costs of production and technology, are likely to change regularly if not continuously. This means that an equilibrium price is likely to be short-lived. Equally, producers usually lack adequate information about the market to predict the equilibrium price precisely. Nevertheless, we can usefully view the competitive market as an evolving process in which firms attempt to position their products and set their prices so as to sell their outputs profitably and expand their businesses. Any changes in the conditions of demand and supply must lead to a new equilibrium price in the market which the competitive process leads firms to seek out.

The firms most successful at seeking out this price are those most likely to succeed over the long term as they carry fewer stocks of finished products and do not alienate consumers by a failure to supply.

Price and managerial objectives

Pricing is driven by managerial objectives. The precise objectives pursued by management ultimately determine the kind of pricing strategy that is adopted. As we saw in the previous chapter, management might pursue profit maximization, corporate growth maximization, sales revenue maximization, or they might attempt to maximize their own sense of well-being (perhaps subject to a minimum profit requirement to keep shareholders contented). Equally, firms may not maximize anything, preferring instead to achieve a satisfactory outcome to a range of objectives (a satisficing policy). In some industries, notably where there are state-run firms, the target could be breakeven or perhaps involve a negative mark-up. That is to say, the price is set so as to produce a politically acceptable rate of loss, the burden of which is borne by taxpayers. Equally, private sector firms may from time to time adopt for short periods a pricing policy which leads to no profits or even losses, perhaps to win market share or to protect a brand during a cyclical downturn in the economy or to fight off a competitor in the market place. Occasionally, products may be used as 'loss leaders' (for instance, to attract consumers into the store, some goods could be priced very low and displayed in the shop window). Firms also need to keep a wary eye on important considerations in the market, such as the state of current demand, the market growth rate, the stage in the product's life cycle, its price elasticity, and the prices set by competitors.

Whatever objective is being pursued, however, will have implications for pricing. The firm which endeavours to maximize its profits will adopt a different price to one which is more concerned with maximizing its market share or sales (see Chapter 5). This follows from the fact that, in general, firms face downward sloping demand curves. The lower the price the larger the volume of sales and hence the greater the likely market share. By contrast, the more profit-orientated firm may purposely restrict its output to maximize the difference between its sales revenue and supply costs.

Generic pricing strategies

In this section we consider the generic pricing strategies that firms might adopt. It is possible to perceive of firms adopting different pricing strategies as competition in the market alters over time, or for different products. The implications for pricing of competition, the product life cycle and multi-product firms are considered later in the chapter.

Four generic pricing strategies are discussed here, namely:

- Marginal cost pricing.
- Incremental pricing.
- Breakeven pricing.
- Mark-up pricing.

Marginal cost pricing

Marginal cost pricing involves setting prices, and therefore determining the amount produced, according to the marginal costs of production, and is normally associated with a profit-maximizing objective.

A firm maximizes its profits when the difference between total sales revenue and total supply costs is at its greatest. This is equivalent to the output level where marginal cost (MC) equals marginal revenue (MR), as explained earlier in Chapter 3.

In a highly competitive market the price charged by a firm in the industry must be identical to the prices charged by the large number of competitors. Hence, the firm faces a perfectly elastic demand curve in the sense that any attempt to price above the market price, even by a very small margin, will result in a total collapse of the firm's sales. This means that when price is set at the market price, the marginal revenue is constant and equal to this price. Therefore, the profit-maximizing condition MR = MC results in price being set equal to marginal cost. This is the essence of a marginal cost-pricing strategy in highly competitive markets.

In an imperfectly competitive market where products are differentiated sufficiently so that firms can charge different prices (e.g. as in the colour TV market), the demand curve faced by the individual firm is downward sloping, as is the marginal revenue curve. The condition of MR = MC still determines the profit-maximizing output, but now price is set above marginal cost (see Figures 4.4 and 4.7 in Chapter 4 which deal with pricing in monopoly situations and imperfect competition). Hence, in such markets price is *related* to marginal cost rather than *equal* to it.

Incremental pricing

Marginal cost is the change in total cost from expanding output by *one* unit, while marginal revenue is the incremental revenue arising from the sale of this extra unit. However, because of indivisibilities in many industries it is not realistic to talk about one unit output changes. Instead, the issue is whether to produce a further batch of output or open another shop or bank branch, etc. Also, in many instances the firm's demand and cost conditions at the margin may not be known precisely and they may be too costly to discover. In such cases, a form of marginal cost pricing called *incremental pricing* might be adopted.

> **Incremental pricing deals with the relationship between larger *changes* in revenues and costs associated with managerial decisions. Proper use of incremental analysis requires a wide-ranging examination of the *total* effect of any decision rather than simply the effect at the margin.**

It will be appreciated that fixed costs are irrelevant to both marginal cost and incremental pricing since these costs are 'sunk' and therefore do not change with output (unless the firm is already working at full capacity and therefore output can only be increased by investing, i.e. by incurring more fixed costs). The decision to supply then simply reflects whether the change in total revenue (TR) is greater or less than the change in variable costs (i.e. the marginal or incremental costs from raising output).

A well-known example of incremental pricing involved Continental Airlines in the United States, which in the late 1950s decided whether to add or cancel flights according to whether the increase in TR from a flight covered the incremental cost of the flight. If fixed costs (the aircraft, management overheads, etc.) were ignored and the costs of keeping a plane parked at an airport were reflected in the opportunity costs of not flying, it made sense to fly a route even where losses resulted. In other words, a *smaller* loss resulted from flying than not flying. Hence, Continental's operating rule was, in effect, 'does the flight at least cover its incremental costs?' Where a flight more than covered these costs but still operated at an overall loss, it of course made a useful contribution towards the fixed costs.

This example raises the thorny subject of allocation of fixed costs. In modern accounting, rules exist for allocating the costs (notably through a method called *absorption costing*) so as to minimize distortion of resource allocation. Nevertheless, some firms still cling to broad brush rules such as allocating overheads according to a product's share in total revenue or total output. This is not an academic issue. The extent to which a product bears fixed costs affects its total costs and hence its viability. Loading higher overhead costs onto high-revenue earners or high-volume products (successful products!), produces smaller margins for these products, and may even lead to their eventual withdrawal from the market. Once these products no longer exist, the overheads then must be allocated to the remaining products, putting their viability in jeopardy. All of the pricing strategies detailed in this chapter rely for their success on sound costing systems.

Breakeven pricing

Breakeven pricing requires that the price of the product is set so that total revenue earned equals the total costs of production.

Using simple arithmetic, we can calculate the breakeven output. For instance, if we are told that the unit sale price of a good is £20 per item and that the variable costs are £9 per unit with fixed costs of £330,000, the breakeven sales level is:

At breakeven:

total revenue (TR) = total costs (TC)
$\qquad\qquad\qquad\quad$ = fixed costs (FC) + variable costs (VC)

Therefore:

$£20 \times$ quantity (q) = $£330,000 + £9 \times q$

Hence:

$$q = 330,000/11$$
$$= 30,000 \text{ units.}$$

A typical breakeven point is illustrated in Figure 6.2. The breakeven, q, output (where TR = TC) is greater than that at which profit is maximized, i.e. q^*.

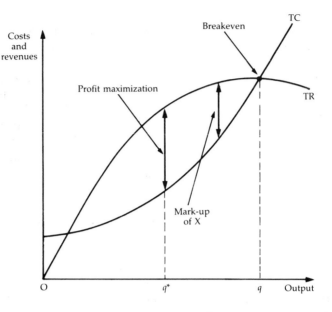

Figure 6.2 Pricing strategies compared

Like marginal cost pricing, breakeven pricing requires a detailed knowledge of the firm's cost and demand conditions. In practice, firms may only be able to identify with reasonable accuracy a 'breakeven area' rather than a breakeven point. Also, breakeven analysis is much more complicated for multi-product firms, a subject to which we turn later in the chapter.

Mark-up pricing

Mark-up pricing is similar to breakeven pricing, except that a desired rate of profit is built into the price (hence this pricing is also sometimes referred to as cost-plus pricing, full-cost pricing or target-profit pricing).

The particular mark-up will be what management consider appropriate or necessary to achieve a profit which satisfies the shareholders. This might be equivalent to what the capital could earn if employed elsewhere in its next best alternative use (i.e. a 'normal' profit). For example, if the next best use generates a rate of return of 8% then the capital would have to earn at least 8% in its current use or it would pay to invest elsewhere. It should be appreciated that mark-up pricing tends to lead to stable prices when costs are not changing much and to large price increases at times of inflation.

When following a mark-up pricing strategy a firm needs to estimate the average variable cost of producing and marketing the product. This requires some view as to the level of output. It is common practice to take a level equivalent to between 70 and 80% of capacity working, unless there are good reasons to choose an alternative. To this average variable cost is then added the average fixed cost to calculate the average total cost. A mark-up figure is then added which represents the required profit margin.

In notation:

$$m = (P - C)/C$$

where m is the mark-up, C is the fully allocated average cost, and $P - C$ is the profit margin.

The price, P, is then given by:

$$P = C(1 + m)$$

For example, assuming a desired mark-up of 25%, the average variable cost per unit at £10 and the fixed cost per unit at £6, such that $C = £16$, the selling price, P, is equal to £16(1 + 0.25) = £20.

A strategy of mark-up pricing tends to be simpler to implement than marginal cost pricing because management do not need to know the relevant marginal revenues and costs. Also, to the unwary it appears to guarantee the desired profit! However, it is unlikely to generate *optimal* profit-maximizing prices since it ignores demand completely. There is no guarantee that the output produced will all be sold at the particular mark-up price or even that the output is sufficient to satisfy demand. This highlights the risk associated with pricing based on an arbitrary profit margin rule. Prices may not necessarily clear the market and there is the further danger that the price set will be undercut by the competition. Like all cost-based pricing strategies, it could be argued that mark-up pricing starts at the wrong point. It will usually make more sense for management first to discover the maximum price at which the product could be sold (the price set by competitors?) and then work backwards, determining what costs are permissible to leave an adequate profit margin *at that price* (this is known as 'backward cost pricing').

In practice, most firms which claim to use a mark-up pricing policy also consider the implications for demand. If they didn't they would not survive for long! Although mark-up pricing is still widely used, since the early 1970s there has been evidence that firms have become much more flexible in their pricing strategies. In an ever increasing competitive environment, mark-ups are being varied to reflect demand conditions. This has led to prices which are closer to those which would be determined by a profit-maximizing price. Where firms apply higher mark-ups to products which are less price sensitive (i.e. less price elastic), mark-up pricing approximates the profit-maximizing rule.

Reviewing pricing strategies

With reference to Figure 6.2, we can highlight the implications for prices and outputs resulting from the various pricing strategies. It will be observed that, provided that the desired mark-up, X, falls short of the profit-maximizing level, the firm's output will be lower than it would be if working to a breakeven rule but higher than under the profit-maximizing rule. Given a downward sloping demand curve this means that the price will be lower than under a profit maximization strategy but higher than where a breakeven policy is pursued.

Pricing and the competitive environment

The nature of the market in which the product is sold will have a major influence on the pricing policy adopted. As we saw in Chapter 4 markets can be conveniently divided into four broad kinds:

- Perfectly competitive markets.
- Monopoly markets.
- Monopolistically competitive markets.
- Oligopoly markets.

We discuss briefly below the appropriate approach to pricing in each of these market forms.

Pricing in perfectly competitive markets

In perfectly competitive markets the supplier is a *price-taker*.

That is to say, since each firm's product is indistinguishable from the products of all other competitive firms the consumer buys only on the basis of price. Commodity markets come closest to this type; for instance, tin producers tend to have to accept the going world price for their tin, otherwise they are undercut by other suppliers. Where perfect competition exists, management has no discretion regarding the individual firm's pricing strategy. Survival decrees that the output must be sold at the market price, the price charged by competitors.

Pricing in monopoly markets

In a monopoly situation, the firm is a *price-maker*.

Thus as markets become less competitive – i.e. as the degree of monopoly power of the firm increases – suppliers will have more discretion when setting prices. Raising the price will reduce demand but not completely destroy it. Price elasticity of demand now becomes an important consideration in price setting. The less price elastic (i.e. the more insensitive) the demand for the product the greater will be the firm's market power and the greater the management's freedom to set prices. Hence, the monopolist has more freedom than a firm in a competitive market to determine its price. The actual price set by the monopolist will depend upon what objective is being pursued. For example, a sales maximization strategy, perhaps to preserve the monopoly position by deterring new competitors, implies a lower price than a short-term profit maximization goal. This type of strategy is commonly referred to as *entry-limit pricing*.

Pricing in monopolistically competitive markets

Perfectly competitive and pure monopoly markets are rarely found – most firms are subject to some competition but to a lesser extent than would arise under perfect competition. More commonly, most firms are faced with a large number of competitors producing highly substitutable products, such that an attempt to achieve product differentiation is a dominant feature of the market place. This situation, referred to as monopolistic competition, means that firms still have some control over the price of their output. Firms cannot sell all they want at a fixed price, nor would they lose all their sales if they raised prices slightly. In other words, most firms face downward sloping demand curves.

In monopolistically competitive markets, firms put considerable marketing effort into segmenting their markets and thereby reducing competition.

Pricing in oligopoly markets

When markets are monopolistically competitive, firms are more likely to make decisions without explicitly taking into consideration competitive reactions. While this may be more appropriate for some industries than others, it is less applicable in an oligopoly market where an individual firm's actions are very likely to provoke a competitive reaction.

For example, when Ford raises the price of its popular Escort range of cars, it knows that demand will be affected but it can also be confident that because of brand loyalty sales (hopefully) will not collapse. Also, firms in oligopolistic industries may price to forestall new entrants. For instance, if Ford suspects that competitors will be able to supply the Escort-type market at a unit cost of £8,000, this will set a limit to the price of the Ford Escort (another form of entry-limit pricing).

In oligopoly markets it is crucial to know how competitors are likely to react to a price change. Will they follow suit or not? Or will they react in some other way, for example with an extensive advertising budget to preserve their market share? Oligopoly markets, therefore, reflect various competitive strategies in which price may or may not be a critical variable. As also observed in Chapter 4, they are also prone to *collusion* and the formation of cartels (if firms co-operated in setting their prices uncertainty faced by firms would be reduced) and to *price leadership*. In markets where there is a price leader, pricing policy may have similarities to pricing in highly competitive markets with the going rate set by one firm being important and with less attention paid by other firms to their own demand and cost functions.

The marketing mix and the product life cycle

The marketing mix

Pricing strategies require the integration of pricing into a wider *marketing mix*, which takes into account other factors than price which determine demand. Some firms may be reluctant to change price because of the uncertain effects on rivals' actions, so the other marketing variables take on added importance. At the same time, research suggests that consumers may only have a vague idea of the price of products they buy, which appears to relegate the importance of price in demand, though it does not remove it altogether. At the very least pricing should complement the other factors in the marketing mix.

In developing an effective marketing strategy, marketing professionals draw attention to the importance of the following 'four Ps':

- Product.
- Place.
- Promotion.
- Price.

Together the four Ps determine what is called the 'offer' to the consumer.

Product

The product raises the issue of consumers' perceptions of the product's characteristics. The perceived value or utility to the consumer rather than the supplier's costs of provision becomes the key to pricing strategy with non-price factors used to increase the perceived value. Whereas breakeven and mark-up pricing emphasize costs as the basis of price, attention to the marketing mix places the emphasis more squarely on demand, with products perceived to be of higher quality or status than the nearest competition-attracting 'premium prices'. When the founder of Revlon cosmetics proclaimed that 'In the factory we make cosmetics, in the store we sell hope!', he was well aware that his marketing success had opened the road to high profit margins.

Place

Place relates to the distribution of the product. How well a product is distributed is important to its success. Hence, successful suppliers put considerable time and resources into distributing the product effectively. Can the product be moved quickly from warehouse stores to retail outlets? Is the product best displayed in supermarkets? Are distribution costs controlled to enable competitive pricing? A complicating factor for producers of a consumer good lies in the growing power of the retailer. A marked trend of the post-war period has been the manufacturer's loss of control over his own product's marketing at the point of sale.

Promotion

Product promotion involves effective marketing including the provision of adequate credit (very important for consumer durables) and advertising. Brands with intrinsically average quality but high advertising budgets may achieve premium prices. Advertising shapes consumers' perceptions of the product and increases consumer demand at all prices. Thus more can to be sold at a constant price or the same amount at a higher price, leading to healthier margins (i.e. there is scope for *margin management*). There is also some evidence that successful advertising by increasing market segmentation reduces price sensitivity. It therefore enables suppliers to gain a *differential advantage* by distinguishing themselves from the competition. In effect, the firm gains a 'quasi-monopoly' position. Segmentation and differential advantage involve aspects of product positioning, in which price is just one variable contributing to that positioning.

Price

Product, place and promotion all leave their mark on both a firm's demand and cost relationships. Price has to fit with the remainder of the marketing plan because together they determine the product's 'positioning' in the market place. For instance, BMW and Lada both produce cars but if their cars were perceived to be the same by consumers, competition would centre on price and Lada would gain market share at the expense of BMW. The fact that this does not occur is in part a tribute to the marketing of the BMW cars. BMW is popularly perceived to produce cars of high quality and high status. By contrast, the Lada is judged to be of poor quality and low status, hence it sells very largely on price alone. There are no prizes for guessing where the highest profit margin is earned. Over the years BMW has successfully cultivated an image which gives it 'brand loyalty'. The brand loyalty relating to Lada is almost certainly much smaller and more vulnerable to competition. The Lada distributor in the United Kingdom therefore faces a threat from *brand switching* and must price very competitively in order to retain customers.

In the motor industry, price has become a leading indicator to consumers of supposed quality. This is also especially true for services, where what is being bought cannot be easily inspected before purchase. For example, in the marketing of management training courses, high-priced courses are positioned by their providers as high-quality, elitist events. Consumers may be excused for assuming that it is more worthwhile to participate in a highly priced course provided by a leading business school than a cheaper alternative at the local technical college.

The positioning of a good or service in the market has major implications for pricing policy. There is no point in marketing a high-quality product and then selling it at a down-market price. Equally, a product perceived to be of low value must be priced accordingly. Where a firm is competing for consumers and wants to earn high profit margins, it must try to ensure that its and its competitors' 'offers' as far as possible are not compared on price alone.

The product life cycle

A further important factor in pricing strategy is the *product life cycle*. Products usually undergo life cycles covering the period from their inception in the market to their eventual withdrawal. A typical life cycle is illustrated in Figure 6.3.

The notion of the product life cycle raises important issues for pricing since it implies that there may be a case for adopting different strategies at each stage of the cycle. Notably, when a product is launched the following two broad pricing strategies can be adopted.

1. 'Promotional' or 'penetration pricing' in which the price is set low to enter the market against existing competitors, attract consumers to the new product, and gain market share.

Consequently there is a more rapid diffusion of the product in the market and as output rises unit costs fall. Penetration pricing makes most sense where unit costs fall dramatically and quickly as output rises due to economies of scale and experience curve effects.

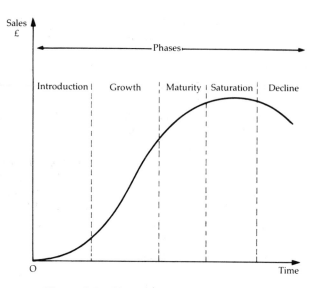

Figure 6.3 Phases of the product life cycle

At the early stage of the product life cycle initial losses from pricing low might be financed in multi-product firms by mature cash-generating products ('cash cows'). In single-product firms the strategy requires sympathetic and strong-nerved investors and bankers.

By contrast, in the growth stage of the product life cycle, price may have ceased to be a primary consideration for consumers, other aspects of the marketing mix having taken over in promoting the product. In the maturity stage, there is little point in pricing to gain market share and the emphasis instead is likely to be on *profit contribution*. Lastly, in the final stage of the product life cycle, as the product declines in popularity prices may have to be cut to maintain demand and hence margins shrink.

2. A 'skimming policy' arises when price is set high initially to cover large unit costs in the early stage of the product life.

This policy will be attractive where a new product has a monopoly position in the market for a short period. Producers attempt to maximize the present value of the future profit stream by charging a monopoly price in the early years of the product's life and a lower price later once competitive pressures begin to emerge. The high initial price under a skimming policy implies a lower rate of growth of sales than under a penetration pricing strategy. Hence, it will be more appropriate where unit production costs do not decline significantly as output rises.

Whichever pricing strategy is adopted for a new product, it is important to recognize that the price set at the outset will have implications for longer-term pricing, especially in the case of consumer products. Consumers tend to relate their perceptions of the product to the initial price.

In the same way as there are product life cycles, there are also *market-power life cycles* with a firm's ability to price high varying over time depending upon its competitive position in the market for its entire product range. When a firm is fighting to survive, prices will reflect this and be aimed at increasing immediate cash flow. This may also be so in the recession period of a trade cycle.

The economics of price discrimination

Many producers sell their products at different prices to different customer groups for various reasons. For example, quantity discounts may be given for bulk purchases or to retain a valued customer. Prices may reflect differences in transport costs to different markets. Also, where demand fluctuates with seasons or time of day, marginal supply costs may justify some form of peak-load pricing (considered fully later in the chapter). In all these cases price varies essentially because the costs of supplying different consumers vary. However, economists reserve the term *price discrimination* specifically to identify only those circumstances where different consumers exhibit different responses to prices; i.e. where there are different price elasticities. Such a situation justifies differential pricing for the *same product*.

Definition of price discrimination

Price discrimination represents the practice of charging different prices for various units of a single product when the price differences are not justified by differences in production/supply costs.

The critical factor for successful price discrimination is the ability of the firm to control its own prices. In other words, there must be imperfect competition such that an effective barrier exists to stop consumers from being able to buy the product at a low price and to on-sell at a higher price (hence the reason why low-priced airline tickets are usually non-transferable). Also, there must be different price elasticities of demand in the various markets. These differing elasticities may reflect different preferences, information and perceptions of the product, and incomes and tastes. Where different price elasticities exist there is scope for price discrimination. An obvious example is the pricing of seats on public transport. The cost of transporting a child is the same as transporting an adult but the demand elasticities are likely to differ.

Price discrimination, in practice, is a matter of degree. Thus, three possible strategies may be identified. These are referred to as follows:

- **First-degree price discrimination.**
- **Second-degree price discrimination.**
- **Third-degree price discrimination.**

We briefly comment on each below.

First-degree price discrimination

At the extreme it is possible to conceive of a producer who sells each unit of output separately, charging a different price for each unit according to the consumer's demand function. Imagine a situation where, if a consumer is willing to pay 60p for a chocolate bar then that is what he or she is charged. Another consumer willing to pay only 30p would be charged that amount and so on. Since all consumers pay for each unit of consumption a price which just reflects the marginal utility (i.e. satisfaction) they get from the product, the result is the transfer of all of the *consumer surplus* to the producer (for an explanation of consumer surplus see page 22). Although attractive to the producer, price discrimination of this intensity would require the producer to have a detailed knowledge of each consumer's demand function. Hence, what is known as *first-degree price discrimination* is of theoretical interest rather than practical value.

Second-degree price discrimination

A more useful approximation, *second-degree price discrimination*, involves charging a uniform price per unit for a specific quantity or block of output sold to each consumer. This policy extracts part but not all of the consumer surplus and is found where demand can be metered, as in the pricing of gas, water and electricity, or usage monitored, for example where computer time or xerox machines are rented.

Third-degree price discrimination

Most frequently found is *third-degree price discrimination*, which simply involves charging different prices for the same product in different segments of the market.

The markets may be separated in the following number of ways:

- **By geography** – as when an exporter charges a different price overseas than at home.

- **By type of demand** – as in the market for, say, butter where demand by households differs from the bulk purchase demand of large catering firms.

- **By time** – with a lower price charged for off-peak periods (as in the case of the electricity and telephone sectors).

- **By the nature of the product** – as with private dental care with differential pricing where if one patient is treated he or she is unable to resell that treatment to someone else.

By charging differential prices to the various market segments for the same product the so-called *price discriminator* will be able to increase his total profits above the level that would have existed in the case of uniform pricing. This is because he is soaking up as much consumer surplus as possible (and hence transforming it into *producer surplus* – i.e. higher profit margins for himself!).

For all forms of price discrimination to be successful it is essential that arbitrage cannot occur. Otherwise, consumers buying the product at a lower price could capitalize by selling it in the higher-priced market. This would boost the supply in this market and reduce prices until they were eventually equal in the two markets and the scope for arbitrage ceased to exist. We can now understand why car manufacturers are keen to prevent the re-import of cars sent to foreign markets for sale at lower prices!

Before adopting a price discrimination policy it is important to consider wider effects. British motor manufacturers selling cars cheaper on the continent than at home has led to consumer resentment and a referral to the Monopolies Commission. Firms contemplating price discrimination need to consider not only whether it is technically feasible but its wider impact on both their image and the threat of state intervention.

Pricing in multi-plant and multi-product firms

So far we have been primarily concerned with the pricing of one product by a firm which appears to produce its output in one location. In practice, however, most firms of any real size produce a range of products and on more than one site. This raises interesting questions for pricing and for the resulting distribution of production across the firm. The existence of more than one production point also facilitates price discrimination between different geographic areas served. This will be especially so where the production occurs in different countries and national markets are protected by import controls.

The multi-plant firm

Where a firm's output of the same product is produced on more than one site, the profit-maximizing output rule, that marginal supply costs must equal marginal revenue, is unchanged, but in this case marginal cost is the *sum* of the separate plants' marginal costs and production must be allocated between the plants so that the marginal supply cost at each plant is identical.

This situation is illustrated in Figure 6.4, where the firm is assumed to have two plants, A and B, which both produce an identical product. Profit maximizing occurs where the firm's total output Q_T is divided between the two plants in the proportions q_A in plant A and q_B in plant B. This follows since profit maximization requires cost minimization and if MC_A did not equal MC_B costs could be further reduced by shifting some output from the higher-cost to the lower-cost plant.

Where the firm produces multi-products on different sites the production and pricing problem is more complicated.

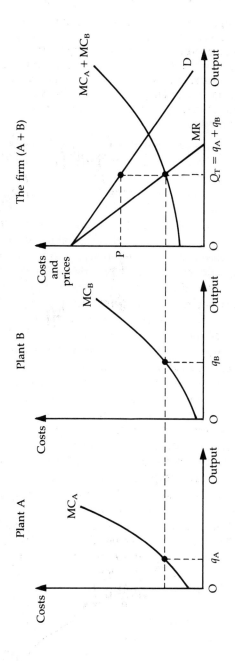

Figure 6.4 Pricing in a multi-plant firm

The multi-product firm

When producing and pricing a product, the multi-product firm has to take into consideration not only the impact on the demand for that product of a price change (its own price elasticity of demand) but the impact on the demand for the other products in the firm's range (the relevant cross-price elasticities). In other words, pricing now involves obtaining the desired rate of return from the full product range rather than individual products.

Such *full-range pricing* means that the firm may be content to earn little or no profit on certain products, preferring to use them as 'loss leaders' to attract consumers who then (hopefully) buy the higher-profit items. This has been for a long time the strategy of some supermarkets. They make very slim margins on basic goods such as bread and potatoes, which because they are widely sold in other shops have a relatively high price elasticity, making their profits on higher-margin (i.e. lower demand elasticity) goods, such as items sold at the delicatessen counter. Contrast this with the attitude to pricing in the post-war British motor cycle industry where the objective was to earn healthy profits from each model, and the price was set accordingly. The British industry's market disappeared within a decade as Japanese competitors undercut the UK producers' prices. The Japanese goal initially was market share or longer-term profits from selling a full product range.

In multi-product firms the products can be complementary, such as Kodak which sells cameras and film, or substitutes, such as Procter and Gamble's detergents. In both cases demand for the products is interrelated. This means that profit maximization requires that the output levels and prices of the products produced are determined *jointly* (in some firms the marketing departments of the various products may compete to increase efficiency and drive down costs, but this risks ignoring the high cross-price elasticities with damaging results for overall profitability).

In addition to demand interdependencies, multi-product firms may have production interdependencies. The most obvious example relates to the production of by-products. In such cases, complex 'joint-costing' rules must be introduced and *economies of scope* recognized (cost reductions resulting from supplying together two or more products). Products can be produced jointly in fixed or variable proportions. The classic example of production in fixed proportions is beef and hides which are produced equally. Hence, the costs of supply cannot be meaningfully apportioned between the two outputs.

Where joint products can be produced in variable proportions then the profit maximization rule requires that the marginal revenue from each output is equated with its own marginal cost, with due cognizance given to any demand interdependencies.

Transfer pricing

Large-scale multi-product, multinational firms are often decentralized by being split into semi-autonomous divisions, with each responsible for its own price and output decisions as well as profit performance. However, decentralization brings with it problems of resource allocation, one aspect of which is the pricing of products which are transferred between divisions. This gives rise to the need for *transfer pricing* and the problem of determining the transfer price which maximizes overall company profits. For example, it may be possible for one division to raise its own reported profits by raising the transfer price but this may be at the expense of profits made by the receiving division. In such situations the general answer to the transfer-pricing problem is that the product being transferred between divisions should be priced at marginal cost.

Furthermore, when divisions are located in different countries with different tax systems, transfer pricing can be used to redistribute profits between countries in order to minimize the overall tax liability. This could be achieved, for example, in situations where one country, A, has a high profits tax relative to another country, B. By setting the transfer price artificially low in country A, the profits could be realized in country B. It should be noted, however, that under fiscal regulations such arrangements are usually illegal – though they are also difficult to police.

Peak-load pricing

Where the demand for a product varies over time it can pay to introduce a form of discriminatory pricing called *peak-load pricing*. In this case, the major factor leading to differentiated prices is the differences in supply costs over time, i.e. the marginal cost of supplying the product or service is much lower at off-peak times when there is spare capacity, and much higher at peak times when there is congestion. The higher peak-time costs may be due to several factors as follows:

- **Diminishing returns** and hence higher short-run marginal costs.
- The need to use **more expensive inputs** to satisfy peak-time demand.
- The whole of the **capital costs** of the additional capacity needed to satisfy peak-time demand being attributable to the peak user.
- **Externalities**; for example, rush-hour traffic congestion imposes external costs on other travellers such that the marginal cost to *society* as a whole rises.

Peak-load pricing is used extensively not only in public transport, but in electricity and gas supply, the postal system and telecommunications, and by travel companies and hotels which charge much less for the same holiday or room 'out of season', e.g. the pricing of 'winter weekend breaks'.

When differentiated pricing is introduced in this way some consumers will alter their demand pattern. For example, they may change to travelling off-peak or they might install an off-peak electricity meter. This is desirable as it smooths out demand thus reducing congestion in peak periods. However, if peak-load pricing causes such a shift in consumer behaviour that the previous off-peak period now becomes a peak period, prices will have to be adjusted further and this may mean less differentiated pricing with off-peak users also bearing some of the capital costs.

Pricing policy and the role of government

All market economies have some state intervention in pricing in the form of taxation and subsidies, and direct controls, such as regulations and licensing. Also, in many countries state-owned industries exist at central and local government levels and some decision must be taken on the pricing of their outputs.

Taxes and subsidies

In a private market the price consumers are willing to pay reflects the benefits they receive from marginal consumption. However, in some cases the price consumers are willing to pay may not accurately reflect the true *social* benefits and costs of the consumption – i.e. there are externalities – in which case the price could be altered through taxes and subsidies. For example, coal-fired power generation causes major pollution, so it could be discouraged by imposing a pollution tax (based on the principle that the polluter should pay). Equally, in so far as public transport has wider social benefits by reducing congestion on the roads, demand for it can be encouraged by state subsidies to keep prices low.

It is important to appreciate, however, that only some forms of taxation have an effect on the pricing decision. For example, for a profit-maximizing monopoly a tax on corporate profits should not affect price or output because neither marginal revenue nor marginal cost is affected. The tax simply removes some of the monopolist's excess profits or economic rent.

Taxes on products do affect prices and outputs. The price to the consumer is raised, which will affect demand depending on the price elasticity of the product. A subsidy has the opposite effect by reducing the price, though not necessarily by the full amount of the subsidy. Just as the supplier may have to absorb some of the tax to retain demand, so the producer might absorb some of the subsidy.

Direct price controls

Government direct controls on pricing arise out of prices and incomes policies, anti-monopoly and restrictive practices legislation, and other forms of regulation and licensing. The latter has grown in importance in the United Kingdom in recent years following the privatization of major public utilities, namely telecommunications, gas, electricity and water industries. The monopoly suppliers now operate under licences granted by the state, which lay down, amongst other things, price regulations.

Rate-of-return regulation is ultimately an indirect form of price regulation since the price charged is an important variable in determining profits. Where the price is directly or indirectly regulated, competition must centre on some other aspect of the marketing mix. In airlines, for example, where prices are heavily regulated, competition is often focused on the level of service, in-flight catering and movies, speed of the check-in desk, and who flies the most modern aircraft at the peak demand times.

Pricing in the public sector

Although many of the issues raised so far, notably peak-load pricing, are relevant to the public sector, pricing in the public sector raises certain unique issues. To begin with, the public sector may well have different objectives since it is concerned with the wider *public interest* rather than profits. If this is so, state enterprises should set their prices with an eye to the marginal social benefits (MSB) from the additional output and the marginal social costs (MSC) of producing that output. The MSB reflects the benefits to the immediate consumer plus any external benefits (wider social gains) and the MSC is calculated to reflect not only the normal marginal costs – wages, raw material costs, etc. – but any external (social) costs, such as environmental effects. By pricing in this way, a public utility maximizes the difference between the social benefits of production from the output and the social costs of producing that output. The result, however, may be losses which have to be met through taxpayer subsidies and taxation distorts employment, investment and spending decisions. Also, subsidies imply a welfare transfer between payers of taxes and the recipients of subsidized services. Why should all taxpayers subsidize rail users? Is the implied income redistribution equitable?

On the basis of the 'public interest' rule, the public sector should invest and expand output when the marginal social benefit of expanding output exceed the marginal social costs, and should contract production when the marginal social cost exceeds the marginal social benefit. But such pursuit of the 'public interest' through public utility pricing depends upon government correctly assessing the public interest and pursuing it relentlessly. In practice, politicians have tended to interfere with the prices set by nationalized industries to hold down inflation, boost Treasury receipts and preserve jobs even when it has been difficult to perceive a public interest objective. To critics the result has been higher inefficiency in the public sector and lowered managerial morale. A key argument for privatization of state industries has been the removal of damaging political control and the restoration of commercial pricing.

Therefore, the fact that prices are as likely to reflect political considerations as true marginal social costs is a major weakness of state intervention in pricing. This is likely to be an even more acute problem for government services such as social security, education, health and defence. In such services, usually no price is charged, or it is a nominal charge and all or most funding comes from taxation. For example, in the United Kingdom most medical care is free to the user within the National Health Service (NHS). Even where charges are made, for example for NHS medicine prescriptions, they are not related to consumption but are set politically. Hence, they are more akin to a tax.

Concluding remarks

This chapter has been concerned with pricing policies under differing market conditions. As we have seen, optimal pricing requires a full consideration of both demand and cost conditions. Prices based solely on supply costs (with a fixed profit margin) are unlikely to reflect sufficiently the state of consumer demand and hence are likely to lead either to over-supply and thus unsold stocks, or excess demand and unsatisfied consumers. We have also seen that there is a case for a more flexible approach to pricing where markets with different price elasticities are supplied or where a peak-load problem exists. The pricing formula also becomes more complex in multi-plant and multi-product firms; while pricing in the public sector raises its own peculiar problems associated with the inevitable political pressures public sector managers face. Nevertheless, one common theme has run through the chapter – successful firms are those which gain competitive advantage and price remains an important variable in achieving this advantage. In the next chapter we turn to consider another crucial factor in competitive advantage, profitable investment.

7

Investment appraisal

The essence of investment appraisal

Much of the analysis in earlier chapters has been concerned with helping managers make better use of existing resources so as to obtain competitive advantage. We turn now to consider decisions regarding the expansion of the firm's capacity to produce. In the presence of limited resources managers must arrive at decisions about resource allocation. These decisions may often be quite difficult given that the timescale may be very long between the initial capital outlay, the recovery of the cost and the movement into profit. Because capital expenditures impact upon the scale, efficiency and structure of a firm, they are of central importance to any management decisions. For example, a well-planned series of outlays can transform the nature and fortunes of a company. Successful investments can turn a loser into a winner, while foolish investments can rapidly sink a firm that might otherwise have remained healthy.

In this chapter we lay the foundations for an understanding of sound investment appraisal techniques. In particular, we cover the following subjects:

- The investment selection process.
- Estimating cash flows.
- Evaluating and ranking investment projects.
- Undertaking a cost-benefit analysis.

The investment selection process

Five steps of the investment selection process may be identified, as shown in Figure 7.1. These are as follows:

Step 1. **Generation of investment proposals.** This is perhaps the most important step in the investment selection process, since without research and development and exploitation of new products and markets, firms are likely to wither and die. If a firm's managers, employees, advisers and consultants cannot come up with a promising stock of project proposals, there is no way that investment selection techniques will enable a firm to make something out of nothing. The generation of ideas represents the seed corn for future growth and prosperity in all businesses. In terms of strategic planning, it is vital that management develops the creative and stimulating environment which promotes profitable investment proposals.

Step 2. **Determination of the investment budget.** Usually investment is budget constrained in the sense that not all of the generated proposals can be financed. In some cases the budget for capital investment may be determined by a process of consultation or it may be rigidly imposed on the management team from above, as in the case of a holding company determining the budget of a subsidiary. Budgetary control, therefore, fills a central role in investment selection since without a budget little acorns do not grow!

Step 3. **Evaluation and selection of investment projects.** All relevant information concerning the project should be quantified in order to estimate expected cash flows. Various techniques are available to do this, taking into account the degree of uncertainty which may be attached to each project. On the basis of estimated cash flows and associated risk and uncertainty, management can evaluate and select appropriate projects for implementation.

Step 4. **Monitoring of investment performance.** Once the project is implemented it is important to monitor its performance on an on-going basis. This monitoring may be in terms of production flows, control of costs and the generation of revenues, all of which will be under the domain of the

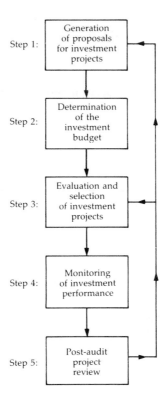

Figure 7.1   The investment selection process

relevant managerial functions, e.g. production, finance, sales, etc. Firms should, of course, monitor project performance on a regular time basis, the actual time period being dependent on the nature of the investment. It is important that if problems are arising, such as cost escalation, appropriate corrective action is taken

Step 5. **Post-audit project review**. Once a project is well established, it is advisable, perhaps after a year or so, to examine in finer detail its performance in the light of initial expectations concerning cash flow, risk, performance, etc. This will ensure a greater likelihood of success when making future investments, thus enhancing corporate profitability in the long run. There are therefore important feedback loops into the generation of proposals (step 1) and into the evaluation and selection procedures (step 3). An *ex post* evaluation may reveal new opportunities to increase profits further. In addition, post-auditing of investments is likely to enhance the overall quality of decision-making and planning. It will also help to tighten internal control systems and ultimately improve the management of future projects.

The above is a simplified representation of the capital budgeting process, but it helps to highlight some of the most important elements and relationships involved.

Estimating cash flows

For each proposed investment project it is necessary to estimate the corresponding cash flows. This is not an easy task since the future is never certain. In addition, some projects may be implemented solely on the basis of the personal objectives of management, as discussed in Chapter 5. Good investment appraisal ensures that all estimates are reviewed carefully in order to minimize any bias.

The following three points should be borne in mind when estimating cash flows:

- **Incremental analysis**. Cash flows for a project should be estimated on an incremental basis, i.e. the difference between the business cash flow with or without the project. For example, if the firm does not install new equipment to produce outputs of sufficient quality which match competitors' products it may end up losing much of its market altogether.

- **The role of tax**. Companies and other businesses pay tax on their profits and hence cash flows should be calculated on an after-tax basis, based on the appropriate marginal tax rate. This should take into account allowances for capital depreciation.

- **Spillover effects**. In calculating the cash inflows and outflows for a particular project, it is important to take account of the extent to which these are sensitive to indirect or what economists call 'spillover' effects. These effects reflect the consequences, both positive and negative, that a particular activity may have on other parts of the business. It may at first sight appear profitable for a firm to introduce a new product line, but it is important that consideration is given to the impact that this may have on other products sold by the same firm. For example, the UK toilet soap industry is dominated by two companies, Procter & Gamble and Unilever. The introduction of a new brand by one or other company may not only affect its competitors' sales but may also impact upon its own sales of existing lines.

Figure 7.2 below shows a typical cash flow profile. In the initial stages of project implementation cash flow is negative. Once sales expand sufficiently, this situation will be reversed, though it may be some time after the actual introduction of the product to the market before revenues more than offset additional outlays. Throughout this cash flow cycle it is important that management continuously monitor performance and take corrective action as required. After cash flow projections have been arrived at for a particular investment, an evaluation of the project must be carried out (a) to determine its worth to the firm, and (b) to enable management to rank and select which investments should be undertaken. There is a

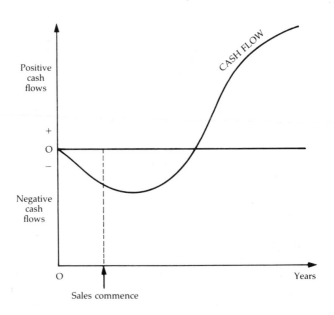

Figure 7.2 Estimating cash flows

variety of methods for doing this, the most important of which we discuss below.

Evaluating and ranking investment projects

Payback method

The simplest approach to evaluating an investment is the *payback method*. Although considered to be less satisfactory than the other methods discussed here, it is, nevertheless, still used widely by businesses in the United Kingdom and elsewhere. Under the payback method investments are judged in terms of how quickly they generate sufficient cash returns to cover the initial investment outlay on the capital project. Projects which, for example, repay within three years are considered preferable to those which take longer to pay back. The major drawback of this method, however, is that it neglects cash flow in later years. The project taking, say, five years to pay back may in fact be more profitable over its life than the project paying back within three years.

The next two methods which we discuss *do* take into consideration cash flows over the entire life of the project. They are the following:

- The net present value method.
- The internal rate of return method.

Both of these methods for evaluating and ranking investment projects are based on the concept of discounting expected cash flows back to the present day so as to obtain their *present value* (PV). This is given by the equation:

$$PV = \sum_{t=1}^{n} \frac{(NCF_t)}{(1 + k)^t}$$

where NCF is the incremental after-tax net cash flow in each year; t represents each year of the life of the investment from the present ($t = 1$) up to a certain number of n years in the future, and k is the discount rate.

We can now use the concept of present value to evaluate investment projects using either the net present value or the internal rate of return methods.

Net present value method

Before calculating the net present value (NPV) of a project the firm must decide the value of the appropriate discount rate (or cost of capital) which is used in the above formula. The ways in which this can be done are discussed in a subsequent section of this chapter. For now we just take the discount rate (k) as given.

If the capital outlays for a project all occur in the current year, the NPV of the stream of future cash flows arising from the project is given by the following:

$$NPV = \sum_{t=1}^{n} \frac{(NCF_t)}{(1 + k)^t} - I$$

where NCF, t and k are as defined in the present value formula above, and I is the initial investment outlay for the project.

The decision about whether investment in a project should be undertaken, therefore, rests on whether or not its NPV is greater than zero. If the NPV is positive the investment has a positive net return in present value terms and should be accepted; if the NPV is negative it should be rejected. Using this simple rule management is able to choose between a range of investment proposals for implementation. Of course, there may be circumstances where an investment would still be undertaken even with a negative NPV, for example where it is an essential part of a project which overall has a positive NPV.

Internal rate of return method

Another measure of the expected profitability of an investment project is referred to as the *internal rate of return method* (IRR). The IRR is defined as the rate of interest that equates the present value of a project's net cash flow to the initial investment outlay. To calculate its value we simply set the NPV for the project equal to zero, i.e.:

$$NPV = \sum_{t=1}^{n} \frac{(NCF_t)}{(1 + IRR)^t} - I = 0$$

The problem therefore is to solve the equation for the value of IRR which produces a zero NPV. This interest rate is the one that equates the present value of the net cash flows to the investment outlay (*I*) – i.e. it is the project's internal rate of return.

Calculation of the IRR is essentially achieved on the basis of a trial and error procedure. First, an arbitrary rate of interest is chosen, and based on this value, the NPV is calculated. If the NPV is positive, this interest rate must be lower than the true IRR so a higher rate must be tried. If NPV is negative, then a lower rate must be used until the correct interest rate which produces a zero NPV is found. At first sight this procedure seems laborious. However, computer packages are readily available to calculate the IRR quickly.

Naturally, managers might be inclined to adopt a 'belt and braces' approach and use both the NPV and the IRR methods when evaluating and ranking investment projects. Using a dual approach, projects are ranked by their IRR and those which have a rate of return which exceeds the risk-adjusted cost of capital are chosen. While the outcome will usually result in the same decision to accept or reject a project as the NPV criterion, it can result in a different decision, for example in cases where cash flows are both negative and positive over a project's life. In general the NPV approach is to be preferred.

A firm with an unlimited capital budget would carry out all the investment projects with a positive NPV since each of these investments adds to shareholders' wealth (presuming, of course, that the expected cash flows materialize!). A problem arises, however, where a firm faces a number of projects, some of which may be interdependent and which cannot all be undertaken because the amount of capital available is limited. In a perfect capital market it would be possible to borrow funds at the opportunity cost of capital to finance any project with a positive NPV at that cost of capital. But in practice capital markets are not perfect, hence projects have to be ranked in order to distribute the firm's limited investment funds amongst the opportunities available. The problem of capital rationing has to be solved. Various solutions to this problem exist which evolve around attempting to maximize the NPVs from the entire investment programme given the limited budget. Two particular methods, though beyond the scope of this book, involve the use of a *profitability index* and *integer programming* (Brealey and Myers, 1990: 85–6, 112).

Cost of capital

Earlier we noted that the discount rate used in the NPV calculation should represent the opportunity cost of capital to the firm taking the investment decision. The cost of capital has to be measured and this raises a number of issues.

In essence, the cost of capital is related to the source of the funds used for investment. A firm may raise funds in a number of ways including the following:

- Loan capital, e.g. bank loans and debenture stock.
- Retained earnings.
- New equity issues.

If only equity finance is used, the return to equity will be the same as the cost of capital. In contrast, if a project is financed entirely by a loan, the cost of capital is the interest rate paid on the loan. In practice, however, firms tend to finance projects using more than one of these sources. When a mixture of loan and equity finance is used, the calculation of the cost of capital is more complex, raising issues concerning the impact of leverage or the gearing ratio (the proportion of debt to equity finance) on the overall cost. Different tax treatments of equity and loan finance further complicate the issue.

The 'traditional' view states that the cost of capital is given by a weighted average of the cost of debt and the cost of equity. Thus the weighted average cost of capital (WACC) is derived. Both the cost of debt and the cost of equity are presumed by some economists to vary with the debt-to-equity (i.e. gearing) ratio, as shown in Figure 7.3. This figure also shows the WACC. It should be noted, however, that the positive relationship between the gearing ratio and the cost of capital was challenged in 1958 by F. Modigliani and M. Miller. They argued that the cost of capital is independent of the gearing ratio. It has to be said, however, that their underlying assumptions used to reach this conclusion are extremely restrictive and the conclusion changes if they are relaxed. In particular, investors may require a higher rate of return to compensate for what they consider to be a greater risk of failure in a more highly geared firm. Also, the Modigliani–Miller thesis assumes that there are no distortions introduced by corporate taxes. This is clearly unrealistic. In the United Kingdom, for example, business loan interest is tax deductible but dividends on equity are not.

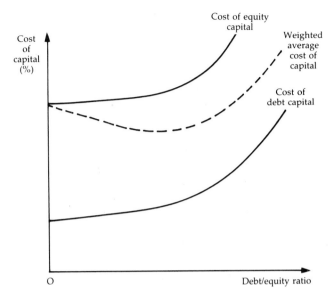

Figure 7.3 The cost of capital

It should also be noted that valuing the cost of equity capital is not problem-free. The cost of equity capital is the rate of return which must be earned on the equity stock in order to ensure that the market price of that stock is unchanged. The estimation of this rate of return may be approached on the basis of two models, namely:

- The dividend valuation model.
- The capital-asset pricing model.

The dividend valuation model

The *dividend valuation model* is based upon the relationship between dividends, market price and the expected return on investment. Different estimation methods exist, but the basic approach is to use the present value of the expected stream of dividends to establish this relationship. The dividend valuation approach makes no explicit reference to the degree of risk attached to the ownership of equity – it is based entirely on the future flow of benefits which the ownership of equity is expected to provide.

The capital-asset pricing model

In contrast, the *capital-asset pricing model* places the valuation of risk at the heart of the analysis. It is concerned therefore with the trade-off between risk and the expected return from equity. This model has its basis in a relatively complex area of financial analysis known as *portfolio balance theory*. Essentially, the model states that the rate of return required by investors is composed of a risk-free rate of return plus a premium which compensates the investor for taking the risk. This risk premium will vary across different shares and will be greater for the shares of those companies whose returns are highly variable than for those whose returns are more stable and dependable. Hence, using this method the degree of risk, given by so-called *beta coefficients*, can be measured for a range of shares. Those shares with a beta greater than 1 are likely to be more risky (the return is more variable) than the overall average risk from investing in the stock market as a whole. Conversely, if the beta value is less than 1 the share concerned is less risky than the market as a whole.

The expected risk-return trade-off reflected in the capital-asset pricing model provides a means of estimating the cost of capital. The practical value of this approach, however, remains a matter for continued debate and empirical testing. The empirical tests which have so far been carried out suggest that the model has some predictive value, but it has been found wanting in the sense that it relies entirely upon the measurement of risk as the determining variable in the cost of capital.

Undertaking a cost-benefit analysis

So far our discussion has been concerned with appraising investment in terms of the resulting net cash flow to the firm. Today, however, more and more private sector firms are conscious of a need to take into account the wider effects of their investments on society, while in the public sector there is a long tradition of what is known as *cost-benefit analysis* (CBA). CBA is concerned with identifying and evaluating both the internal and external consequences of an investment. The internal consequences are the cash flow effects to the firm. The external consequences, or *externalities*, relate to the wider social implications of an investment both in terms of costs and benefits. Some examples of externalities were given earlier in the book.

The following definition summarizes the central concern of CBA:

> Cost-benefit analysis is a practical way of assessing the desirability of projects, where it is important to take a long view (in the sense of looking at repercussions in the distant future, as well as the nearer future) and a wider view (in the sense of allowing for side-effects of many kinds on many persons, industries, regions, etc.); i.e. it implies the enumeration and evaluation of all the relevant costs and benefits (Prest and Turvey, *Economic Journal*, December 1975).

There are no simple rules as to how a firm or public authority should undertake a CBA. Four general stages, however, can be identified, as shown in Figure 7.4.

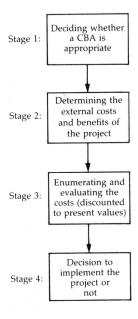

Stage 1: Deciding whether a CBA is appropriate

Stage 2: Determining the external costs and benefits of the project

Stage 3: Enumerating and evaluating the costs (discounted to present values)

Stage 4: Decision to implement the project or not

Figure 7.4   Stages of a cost-benefit analysis (CBA)

Stage 1 is concerned with when a CBA is appropriate. It will, of course, be most appropriate where there are likely to be appreciable externalities from an investment. **Stage 2** is more tricky and requires identifying all of the relevant external costs and benefits. Many of these may be intangible, such as 'noise' and 'beauty'. Evaluating and enumerating these externalities is undertaken in **Stage 3**. The intangible externalities may be particularly difficult to deal with; for example, how do we place a value on someone's loss of peace and quiet? Once all of the benefits and costs over the life of the project are enumerated, they must, of course, be discounted to present values in the same manner as for private investments detailed earlier. Lastly, in **Stage 4**, a decision must be reached as to whether or not to proceed with the investment. Especially in the public sector, the decision is likely to be influenced not only by the figures produced in Stage 3, but by political considerations. The conclusions of public sector CBA studies are sometimes overturned following political pressure from those likely to be most inconvenienced by the investment, for example those whose homes would be most affected by a new motorway link or an airport runway extension.

Concluding remarks

This chapter has been concerned with investment appraisal. Profitable investment is a key factor in the long-term success of any enterprise. Hence it is important that all investments are carefully evaluated. We have seen that a number of methods for appraising investments exist but that the most satisfactory one involves the discounted cash flow technique. This recognizes the significance of the timing of revenues and expenses over the life of a project, whereas the main alternative frequently used, the payback method, places a premium on the net returns in the early years of the investment.

Whichever method of investment appraisal is adopted, it is important to include the relevant costs and benefits. A profit-maximizing firm may be concerned only with the costs to itself of undertaking and financing the investment and the revenues the project generates. In contrast, firms that have become more socially or environmentally aware have to take into account the wider effects of their investments on the community. Cost-benefit analysis is a way of evaluating investments by taking into account *all* of the costs and benefits of a project to the firm and to society. Although initially developed for use in the public sector, it is now playing a greater role in private sector decision-making because of a growing 'environmental awareness'. Public concern with the wider effects of business decisions also lies behind government intervention in the economy, which is the subject of Chapter 9.

8

Understanding the labour market

The essence of the labour market

In many firms the cost of labour is likely to represent a significant proportion of overall production costs. This chapter deals with the factors which determine the amount of labour employed in a firm and the wages paid. The key factor to bear in mind is that the demand for labour is essentially a *derived demand*. People are employed for the output they produce.

The principle of marginal analysis, developed in earlier chapters, can be usefully applied to the labour market. Most firms aim to make and sell goods and services for profit. Obviously, a profit-maximizing firm will not want to pay its employees (including on-costs such as pension provisions and national insurance) more than they add to the value of production. In other words, they will not want to employ someone if the marginal cost to the firm exceeds the marginal revenue generated by the additional employee through more sales. Therefore, and assuming there are no other variable costs than labour (e.g. raw material and component costs), firms wishing to maximize profits will employ more people until the marginal cost of employing them equals the marginal revenue that can be earned by selling the output they produce. Even where firms do not aim to profit-maximize, the principles of marginal analysis are still valuable when discussing the employment decision. They help managers to answer such questions as 'what are the consequences of expanding or reducing our labour force?'

A discussion of employment, especially in economies with highly institutionalized labour markets (e.g. Sweden) cannot, of course, afford to neglect the role of collective bargaining. After a detailed explanation of what economists call *marginal revenue product* theory, the chapter includes, therefore, a consideration of the impact of unions on wages and employment.

It is important to understand that throughout this chapter 'an increase in wages' means an increase in the *real* wage, not simply an increase to offset inflation. It is an increase in the real wage which affects the price of one kind of labour in relation to other types of labour and labour-saving capital equipment.

The demand for labour

For competitive markets, economists link the demand for labour by the individual firm to the marginal revenue product (MRP) of labour. The marginal revenue product is the value added to production by employing one more person. More formally it can be calculated as follows:

$$MRP = MPP \times P$$

where MRP is the marginal revenue product

   MPP is the marginal physical product, i.e. the volume of output added by employing one more person, and

   P is the price at which the output sells.

For example, if the twentieth person employed increased the volume of total output in the firm by 5 units per week, and those units are sold at £30 each, then the MRP of the twentieth employee is $5 \times £30 = £150$. Provided that the weekly cost of employment is less than that amount and there are no other variable costs, the employment is profitable from the firm's viewpoint. If the cost exceeds £150 then it is costing more to employ the person than he or she is contributing to the value of production.

At first, as a firm employs more people, the value each extra person adds to production may rise. This may be because as employment rises people are able to specialize in tasks so increasing the productivity of the total labour force. However, we tend to find that there will come a point at which, as more and more are employed, unless we increase the amount of capital equipment including factory and office space, *diminishing returns* set in. In other words, once a certain employment level is achieved for any given assembly line, shop or office, any further increase in employment leads to a decline in the marginal physical product (MPP). For example, consider a computer department of a firm which currently has twenty employees. The employment of a twenty-first person may lead to a lower MPP. In other words, that person adds less to the volume of production than the twentieth person. Adding a further person, a twenty-second employee, may be associated with a lower MPP than the twenty-first employee and so on. If the firm foolishly carries on employing more people eventually the last person taken on might not be able to find any work to do and therefore the MPP would be zero. If employment continued beyond this point the office would become grossly overcrowded and the *total* volume of production would fall. Now the MPP has become negative!

When deciding the level of employment management should, of course, be concerned not solely with the volume of output added by the marginal employee but also with the price at which that output is sold. Unless the firm can sell all of its additional output at a constant price, the marginal revenue product (MRP) will decline more swiftly than the MPP. This follows since MRP = MPP × price of the product (P). As output rises and firms have to reduce their selling price to sell the additional production, the MRP falls because of both a decline in MPP (due to diminishing returns) and because it must accept the lower price for its product (due to a downward sloping demand curve). We can conceive of a MRP for each type of labour employed from low manual to the highest levels of management.

Table 8.1 shows an example of the relationship between MRP, MPP and price. Thus we note that the MRP of the twelfth worker employed equals £1,500, that for the thirteenth worker is £1,680, for the fourteenth worker £1,300 and so on. The table illustrates the MPP rising at first then falling, and the price of the product falling as output is increased. The MRP curve derived from the data in Table 8.1 is illustrated in Figure 8.1. It will be seen that after the employment level reaches thirteen people the MRP curve begins to decline. If we now assume that all the employees are employed at the same wage of £900 per month, and that there are no other variable costs other than wages, it will clearly pay the firm to

Table 8.1 Calculation marginal revenue product (monthly figures)

Quantity produced (units)	Number of workers employed	Marginal physical product (MPP)	×	Price (per unit)	=	Marginal revenue product (MRP)
550	11	–		–		–
600	12	50	×	30	=	1,500
660	13	60	×	28	=	1,680
710	14	50	×	26	=	1,300
750	15	40	×	24	=	960
780	16	30	×	22	=	660
800	17	20	×	20	=	400
810	18	10	×	18	=	180

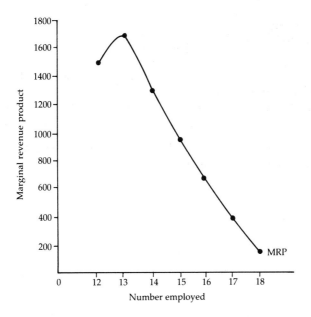

Figure 8.1 The employment decision

employ fifteen people. To employ beyond this number would mean that the marginal cost of employment (the wage) exceeds the value added to production (the MRP). On the basis of this analysis it should be apparent that managers wishing to maximize profits should employ labour (including other managers!) only if their MRP exceeds the cost of employing them.

It should also be apparent that a way to increase employment and/or wages is to increase either the productivity of labour (MPP) or the price of the product produced (*P*) or both. The effect is to raise the MRP of labour. This is illustrated in Figure 8.2 by a shift in the MRP curve to the right. With a given wage of W_1, $N_1 N_2$ more can be profitably employed because the value added to production is increased. Alternatively, N_1 could still be employed but at the higher wage of W_2, or some combination of a higher wage and higher employment, identified along the stretch of the curve between X and Y, could be chosen.

So far we have said nothing about the extent to which the demand for labour might be affected by a change in wages.

The responsiveness of employment to a change in wages can be measured by the *elasticity of demand for labour*

Elasticity of demand for labour $=$ **percentage change in number employed** / **percentage change in the wage rate**

In some cases a wage change may have a significant effect on the demand for labour. In other cases the effect may be insignificant. The extent to which the demand for labour changes in response to a wage change will depend upon such factors as the following:

● The extent to which the labour can be easily replaced by either other labour or capital equipment.

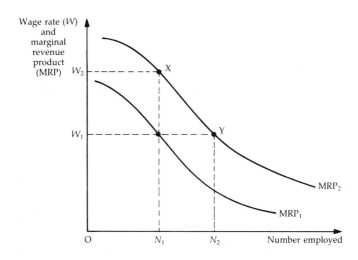

Figure 8.2 Raising labour's marginal revenue product

- The extent to which the firm can pass on increased wage costs to the consumer without appreciably affecting sales of its product. This in turn depends upon the product's *price elasticity of demand* (see pages 29–34).

- The proportion of labour costs in total costs. Wage demands can be most easily accommodated where wages make up only a small part of the firm's total costs (for example, in capital intensive industries such as chemicals).

Using the above formula we can say that the demand for labour is *elastic* when the resulting figure is greater than 1 and *inelastic* when it is less than 1. The procedure for calculation of the elasticity is identical to that for a product's price elasticity, detailed earlier, and again the negative sign, by convention, is ignored.

So far we have been concerned with what is the optimal number of people to employ at a given wage rate. To determine *how the wage rate is derived* we also need to consider the supply of labour.

The supply of labour

At its most basic, the supply of labour is determined by the following:

- **Demographic factors**. The birth and death rate, immigration and emigration, and the participation ratio (the proportion of those of working age who make themselves available for work) are all important in determining the size of the national labour force.

- **The wage rate and other employment inducements, e.g. status, perks, etc**. These factors determine the supply of labour to a particular occupation or firm. Higher wage rates attract more people to a job or occupation.

- **Barriers to entry into different occupations**. Such barriers may be social or cultural (e.g. attitudes to male midwives), legal restrictions or prohibitions (e.g. on women working in coal mines), trade union entry restrictions (such as the pre-entry closed shop), or involve the need for particular qualifications (e.g. graduate-only employment or professional examinations). In addition, ignorance can often be a very potent barrier to labour mobility both between occupations and geographically. Workers may be unaware of job opportunities elsewhere. Barriers to entry and other such restrictions on the supply of labour move the labour supply curve to the left and make it less 'supply elastic' (see below) thus raising the wage (as illustrated in Figure 8.3).

- **Labour mobility.** In a perfect labour market, people would move swiftly and freely from one occupation to another and from one geographic area to another. However, educational and skill requirements may limit occupational mobility. Manual labourers cannot readily be accountants (though if necessary accountants could become manual labourers!). Equally, there could be unemployed accountants in Glasgow and a shortage of accountants in London (or vice versa). Thus we often have in an economy shortages of certain skilled labour alongside a pool of unemployed and great regional variations in employment opportunities. The answer, of course, is to train the unemployed and to adopt a regional policy to level out job opportunities nationally, but both take time and resources. They also require accurate forecasting by government of future job shortages (the record of governments in this respect is generally disappointing).

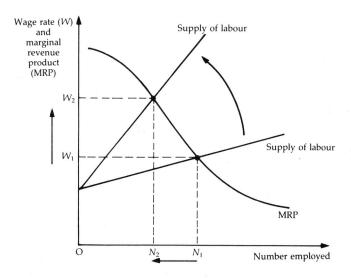

Figure 8.3 The effect of restricting the supply of labour

Leaving aside the other factors which may affect the supply of labour to concentrate upon the wage paid, suppose that the firm is small and when it increases its demand for a type of labour it does not have to increase the wage offered. In other words, the wage is determined in the industry as a whole and the firm pays the going wage rate. In effect the firm then faces a perfectly elastic supply curve of labour. This is illustrated in Figure 8.4, where in a highly competitive labour market the supply curve is horizontal at a wage rate equal to W. Ignoring any other costs of employment, the average and marginal costs of employing labour are constant at that wage. Hence, the firm will employ N amount of labour, i.e. where $MC = MRP$.

In a less competitive situation where a firm may be so large that when it increases its demand for labour it has to pay a higher wage to attract additional employees, the wage paid to the marginal employee will exceed the average wage bill. In other words, the marginal cost of labour rises more quickly than the average cost of employment. Again it will pay the firm to employ labour to the point where the marginal cost of employment equals the value added to sales by the marginal employee, i.e. N workers, given where $MC = MRP$, as illustrated in Figure 8.5. Here W represents the average wage bill to the entire workforce and hence employees

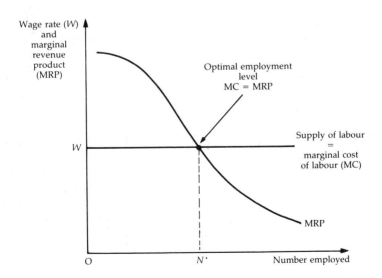

Figure 8.4 Wage determination in a highly competitive labour market

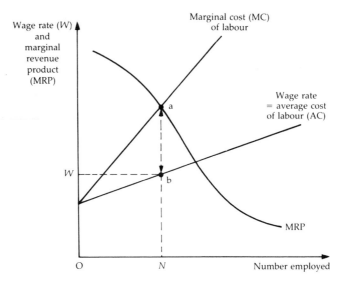

Figure 8.5   Wage determination in a less competitive labour market

are paid less than their marginal revenue product (the shortfall is represented by the distance ab).

The extent to which a firm's supply of labour rises or falls in response to a wage change can be expressed in terms of labour's *elasticity of supply*.

The elasticity of supply of labour is a measure of the responsiveness of the supply of labour to a change in the wage paid.

The elasticity of supply tends to be lower where there are labour shortages and for more highly skilled jobs, for example, dentists. In contrast, the elasticity of supply tends to be high in relatively unskilled jobs where there is surplus labour and where it is relatively easy to move into the occupation, for example office cleaning. This, of course, helps to explain why a senior executive with skills in short supply earns a lot more than a manual labourer in a market economy. The supply of senior executives with the right background is very limited, hence the supply is relatively inelastic. By contrast, there is a large pool of manual labour which forces down wage levels in the manual sector.

The elasticity of labour supply is measured as follows:

Elasticity of labour supply = $\dfrac{\textbf{percentage change in supply of labour}}{\textbf{percentage change in the wage rate}}$

Restrictions on the supply of labour into an occupation tend to make the supply less responsive to wage changes and hence more *inelastic*.

The discussion so far has been concerned with the marginal productivity theory of wage determination in which the demand for labour is a reflection of the marginal revenue product of labour. This approach is obviously most relevant to firms operating in industries where wages are freely negotiated between the employer and employee, such as in small businesses operating in competitive markets and in firms which are non-unionized. In some industries, however, wages may be set by collective bargaining involving a trial of strength between a monopoly seller of labour (the union) and a monopsony or single buyer of labour (e.g. an employers' federation). In this case does the above analysis have any relevance?

Collective bargaining

In 1979 12 million people in the United Kingdom were in trade unions. Ten years later, as a result of unemployment and anti-union legislation, this number had fallen by a third to 8 million. There have been similar trends in certain other countries. Nevertheless, unions are still a major feature of the labour market in the United Kingdom and elsewhere.

A *bargaining theory* of wages suggests that wage determination is a matter of 'negotiation' between 'determined' unions on the one hand and 'intransigent' employers on the other. To managers and union representatives directly involved in wage bargaining this may seem so. Wages are simply the product of a power struggle. However, below the surface of collective bargaining in a market economy the principles of marginal productivity theory may still apply. The forces of demand and supply in the labour market may still be important. In particular, economists suggest that in the long run it is unlikely that unions can raise wages substantially without causing unemployment unless there is a matching increase in the marginal revenue product of labour. As we have already observed, firms will tend to make redundant labour which costs more to employ than it contributes in added value. In certain circumstances a firm might be willing to absorb a wage increase out of profits and may have to in the short term, but over the longer term the firm will attempt to cut costs, for example by substituting capital for labour.

From our earlier discussion we can deduce that unions will tend to be at their strongest in wage bargaining if:

- The firm currently makes more than a normal profit.
- The employer has limited scope to introduce further labour savings.
- Labour costs are only a small part of total costs so that a wage rise can be more easily absorbed.
- Firms can more easily pass on some or all of a wage increase to consumers through higher prices. In other words, when either the demand for the product is rising (e.g. because incomes are rising) or where the price elasticity of demand of the product is low (e.g. in a monopolistic industry such as electricity supply).
- The employer is currently paying a wage which is less than the MRP of labour (for example, as illustrated in Figure 8.5).

Unions can adopt two broad strategies to increase wages:

- Restrict the supply of labour in the market.
- Raise the demand for labour.

The supply of labour can be restricted by closed shop agreements (though in the United Kingdom these have been heavily proscribed in the 1980s by government legislation) or by the imposition of entry qualifications (such as lengthy apprenticeship periods). Turning to the demand for labour, this can be raised, for example, by unions co-operating with employers in productivity deals. Raising productivity increases the MRP of labour (as illustrated in Figure 8.2 earlier) so that higher wages can be paid without lower profits and a loss of jobs.

In collective bargaining employers' organizations act like monopsony buyers of labour. By co-operating rather than competing for labour in the market, employers' federations can work to minimize wage rises. The disadvantage as far as firms are concerned lies in the inflexibility introduced by national wage deals. National agreements fail to reflect local demand and supply conditions leading to localized labour shortages. Hence they often need to be supplemented by wage deals at the firm or plant level. In such circumstances the national deal can become largely irrelevant, or worse it can become the 'going rate' on which inflationary local deals are based.

Concluding remarks

A major objection to the marginal productivity approach to wage determination lies in the in-built assumption that the firm can exactly (or closely) measure the MRP of employees. Often managers will be faced with imperfect information about an employee's productivity and sometimes even about employment costs. The fact that the MRP of labour can only be measured if all other factors of production are held constant complicates the picture. It may prove impossible to separate out exactly the MRP of labour in an integrated production process, especially where employees operate together as teams. Moreover, in some state activities such as the police, where no revenue is earned directly from the work provided, the concept of a MRP does not appear to be particularly useful.

Nevertheless, marginal productivity theory is usually valuable for the general insight it gives managers into the roles of demand and supply in the labour market in determining wages. The analysis underlines the importance of carefully monitoring, even if only in general terms, the value added by extra labour employed. Overmanning, especially in expanding firms where people are taken on in anticipation of work that does not materialize, can quickly, and sometimes disastrously, escalate costs and remove competitive advantage. Indeed, the root of many business failures lies in insufficient attention to labour's MRP. As this chapter has stressed, employment should add *net value* to the firm – labour should be an asset not a liability!

9

Government and business

Introduction

Much of this book is primarily concerned with the firm and its relationship with the markets in which it sells its products and buys its inputs. In this chapter we turn to consider the impact of government on managerial decision-making. In most of the advanced economies today the state has a major role with government expenditure and taxation usually accounting for over 40% of total gross domestic product. The role of government extends beyond the provision of social and economic services, such as education and health care, to establishing and policing property rights, limiting business activities (e.g. to protect the environment), maintaining the infrastructure (e.g. roads and airports), and to providing a safety net in the shape of unemployment, sickness and disability benefits.

A common approach in management when evolving a business strategy is to undertake an analysis of the wider, changing, business environment (we addressed the importance of this briefly in Chapter 1). The study of the wider environment is commonly referred to as a PEST analysis.

A PEST analysis is concerned with identifying and evaluating the *Political, Economic, Social* and *Technological* factors likely to impact on the business in the time period under study (Figure 9.1).

For example, a PEST study for the German car industry in 1991 might have revealed the following factors (the list is far from exhaustive):

- **Political**. German unification and instability in Central and Eastern Europe.
- **Economic**. European integration (the '1992' initiative), German interest rates and the Federal budget deficit.
- **Social**. Migration from former East to West Germany, unemployment in the East, and concern for the environment.
- **Technological**. Continued automation, development of lean-burn engines, and the use of non-rust materials.

By identifying and evaluating the relevant factors likely to impact on the industry through a PEST analysis, management can formulate an appropriate strategy to take advantage of expected opportunities and minimize the impact of anticipated threats.

Obviously, government economic policy will usually be central to a PEST study. Changes in government policy have a major impact not only on the political environment but on the economic, social and technological future that an industry faces. For example, higher interest rates can be expected to slow down economic activity (economic), lead to higher unemployment (social), reduce political support for the government (political), and affect the level of investment in new technology and R&D (technological). An understanding of the nature of government economic policy is therefore crucial to successful managerial decision-making (for a full treatment

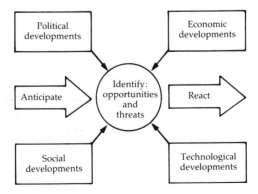

Figure 9.1 A PEST analysis

of government policy at the macroeconomic level, see our companion volume, *The Essence of the Economy*).

This chapter begins by considering the principles underpinning state intervention before moving on to look at the following four key areas of state involvement in the market:

- Macroeconomic policy.
- Industrial policy.
- Competition law.
- Regional policy.

It is important to appreciate the growing significance of European Community (EC) legislation for businesses operating in or trading with the EC. In the past, a discussion of the impact of government on business was likely to have centred upon the role of national governments. French managers were primarily affected by the nature and scope of French state intervention in the economy, British managers with British economic policy and so on. Nowadays, however, the EC is playing an increasing role in the economies of member-countries. This extends to the macroeconomy where the European Monetary System (EMS) and the move towards European economic and monetary union is reducing the freedom of national governments to pursue independent monetary and fiscal policies, and to the microeconomy where the EC is developing European industrial and social policies. At the same time the 1986 Single European Act has introduced a new momentum into European integration helping to sweep away the last barriers to free trade in the EC, especially in services. Frontier checks are being simplified, public procurement programmes liberalized, trade-distorting taxes and subsidies unified and technical standards levelled. Similarly, in North and South America and the Far East new trading agreements are leading to the development of alternative trading blocks.

The principles of state intervention

Economists usually argue that the market is an efficient allocator of resources because it is based on consumer choice. However, there may be certain circumstances where this is not true and the free market does not provide an optimal allocation of resources. This is most likely to occur where there are appreciable *externalities*. We have already had cause to refer to externalities in Chapters 1 and 7. The term refers to benefits and costs which are not reflected in the prices paid by the consumers of the immediate product. Where there are appreciable external costs or benefits, state intervention may take one or other of the following two forms with the objective of encouraging or discouraging consumption:

- Subsidy or taxation of products.
- Prohibiting, licensing or regulating suppliers.

Presuming that government has the objective of maximizing social well-being, consumption should be encouraged of those products which are believed to have significant external benefits (e.g. education and health care), while the consumption of products with external costs should be discouraged (e.g. leaded petrol and noisy aircraft). Therefore, today most governments are involved in one form or another in encouraging the supply of health and education services, usually through direct or indirect subsidies, and discouraging pollution and noise, through regulations, licensing and taxes.

In addition to encouraging or discouraging consumption where there are appreciable external benefits or external costs respectively, governments also intervene in markets for the following other reasons:

- **To regulate the level of economic activity**. Since the Great Depression of the 1930s, governments have tended to believe that the level of economic activity cannot be safely left to market forces. This has applied to both right of centre and left of centre governments, though as might be expected Socialist governments have intervened in the economy with the most relish. In newly developing economies governments have 'planned' investment often using powerful state companies. In the developed economies measures have been adopted to influence investment and consumption with a view to minimizing unemployment while avoiding damaging inflation and balance-of-payments problems.

- **To protect consumers and employees**. Although the consumer is usually considered to be sovereign in market economies, many governments have introduced laws to prevent undesirable practices. Consumer protection law covers such issues as the degree of competition in the market and regulation of advertising. Most countries also have laws to protect the small investor. In the United Kingdom advertising is self-regulated through the Advertising Standards Authority, though if the 'voluntary' code failed government would no doubt intervene directly to prevent misleading advertisements. Governments also have a number of laws relating to the labour market covering the operation of collective bargaining, health and safety at work, equal opportunities, hours of work and statutory minimum wages. Initially, these laws were motivated by a desire to protect workers considered to be at risk of exploitation by unscrupulous employers. By contrast, more recently laws have been introduced, notably in the United Kingdom, to limit the power of trade unions.

• **To alter the free market distribution of income and wealth.** Decisions about the 'right' income and wealth distribution are largely social and political, reflecting the values held by society at the time. In this century democratic governments through progressive taxation and state welfare benefits have become involved in redistributing incomes and wealth from the richer to the poorer sections of the community. In the 1980s this came to a halt in a number of countries because of worries about the impact of high taxes and generous welfare benefits on incentives to work, save and invest. To what extent this is a temporary halt remains to be seen. Also, governments have intervened in the location of businesses through regional policy with a view to redistributing income and wealth spatially.

In the pursuit of these goals governments have introduced a range of policies, details of which are summarized below.

Macroeconomic policy

Government macroeconomic policy is concerned with regulation of the level of economic activity. It therefore impacts directly on businesses by affecting the level of consumer demand and the cost of raising capital. Economies are complex and to many managers fluctuations in economic activity must seem hard to explain or predict. However, managers need to have some understanding of the nature of macroeconomic policy if they are to anticipate successfully the consequences for their trades of policy changes, e.g. a rise in interest rates. It is important to appreciate *why* governments alter interest rates, taxes and spending and *how* the level of economic activity and hence consumer demand are likely to respond. Firms that ignore the macroeconomic environment are likely to be wrong-footed by policy changes.

In essence we can usefully liken an economy to a water barrel, as illustrated in Figure 9.2. The level of water in the barrel represents the level of economic activity. When the water level is constant this is equivalent to a stable level of economic activity. When it rises too quickly and begins to overflow the top of the barrel, this is equivalent to inflation caused by an excessive level of economic activity which pushes up costs and prices and leads to a deterioration in the balance of payments (due to too much demand relative to the domestic supply of goods and services). If the water level falls sharply then this represents a decline in economic activity, which usually leads to unemployment and bankruptcies (due to too little demand relative to supply). Although this is a simple representation of the workings of a modern economy, the central message is clear – the key to good government policy lies in keeping economic activity (the volume of water!) at a level where the economy is fully employed without inflation. In Figure 9.2 this is the level FE which, it should be noted, is below the top of the barrel. Economies need some unemployed resources – there can never be 0% unemployment because a dynamic economy is associated with some unemployment as people move from declining to expanding activities. Putting this another way, operating with a completely full barrel risks a 'spillage' leading to inflation and balance-of-payments difficulties!

You will notice from the figure that there are a number of inflows and outflows from an economy. The 'leakages' are savings (S), taxation (T) and expenditure on imports (M). The 'injections' are investment (I), government spending (G) and revenue from exports (X). In an economy savings, taxation and spending on imports all tend to reduce the level of economic activity, in the sense that there is less income left over to continue circulating around the economy in the form of demand for the goods and services produced. For example, if households save more and spend less, retail sales in the High Street decline, leading to fewer factory orders and so on. In contrast, investment spending, government spending and export sales increase the level of economic activity by adding to total

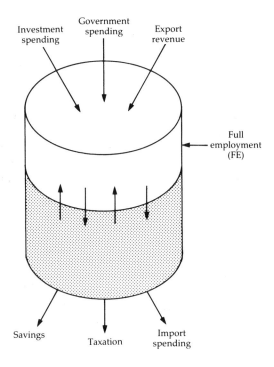

Figure 9.2 Illustrating economic fluctuations

domestic income. For example, new investment in office buildings leads to more orders for the construction industry, more employment in this industry and ultimately more spending in the shops. We can therefore say that just as the level of water in the barrel will vary depending upon the relative size of the inflows and outflows of water, so the level of economic activity is affected by the relative size of the *injections into* and *leakages out* of the economy at any given time. It follows therefore that if:

- $I + G + X$ **equals** $S + T + M$ then the level of economic activity stays constant.
- $I + G + X$ **exceeds** $S + T + M$ then the level of economic activity will rise.
- $I + G + X$ **is less than** $S + T + M$ then the level of economic activity will fall.

From this analysis we can better understand the nature and form of macroeconomic policy. Since 1945 Western governments, notably in the United Kingdom and the United States, have tended to pursue active measures aimed at maintaining the level of economic activity, so if it appeared that the level of economic activity was declining, action was taken to reduce the leakages and increase the injections. For example, in terms of monetary policy interest rates might be cut both to act as a disincentive to save and as an incentive to invest. Alternatively, in terms of fiscal policy government could reduce taxation and increase its own spending. If the level of economic activity appeared to be rising too quickly, leading to inflation, then these policies could be reversed.

In more recent years governments have questioned the value of such intervention and have preferred to rely more on market forces to restore the full employment income level. Government policy has, therefore, been aimed at removing impediments to free-market forces, for example by reducing trade union powers, removing government regulations and lowering tax rates. This policy stance can be broadly described as *supply side policy*. In particular, questions have been raised about the desirability of using public spending and taxation as a means of regulating the economic injections and leakages. Critics have argued that such interventionist policies are often mistimed, leading to an unfavourable impact on economic activity, and that governments vying for votes through more public spending create higher and higher inflation.

In the future, macroeconomic policy in the EC will be constrained by moves towards economic and monetary union. The European Exchange Rate Mechanism (ERM) is an integral part of this movement and links EC currencies to one another through the European Currency Unit (ECU). This limits the freedom of member-governments to pursue independent monetary policies because interest rates have to be set with an eye to maintaining the agreed exchange rate. Also, in the absence of the possibility of devaluing their currency, nations can maintain price competitiveness in international trade only by ensuring that national inflation is not out of line with the rate in other member-countries. This in turn requires more co-ordination in the EC of tax and government spending, thus further reducing the scope for independent reflationary policies. In the 1990s the power of the major EC political bodies (the European Parliament and the Council of Ministers) and of the European civil service (the European Commission) over macroeconomic policy will increase as the role of national governments diminishes. Macroeconomic management will be shaped increasingly on a European scale. The same applies to industrial policy.

Industrial policy

All economic policies have some effect on business, but industrial policy is concerned with those policies which are intentionally adopted by governments with a view to influencing the development of particular industries, sectors of the economy, or firms. Industrial policy impacts on business structure and business restructuring.

A market economy is naturally associated with constant change resulting, in particular, from changes in consumer demands and new technologies. Consequently, at any given time some industries and businesses will be expanding while others are contracting. A problem can arise, however, in terms of *adjustment costs*. The decline of an industry can mean high unemployment and social deprivation, especially when it has been concentrated in particular regions of the economy, for example as in the cases of coal mining and shipbuilding. The rise of a new industry might be held back by inadequate risk capital or labour shortages. For these and related reasons, governments have felt the need to introduce industrial policies to speed up or slow down economic change.

> *Accelerative* **industrial policies are designed to speed up the adjustment process, for example by providing 'soft loans', tax allowances, state subsidies and restructuring grants. By contrast,** *decelerative* **policies are intended to slow down the pace of change, usually through financial aid, and are directed at industries in serious decline. In both cases the state intervention may either be aimed at one firm or selected firms or spread across an industry or business sector.**

The matrix in Figure 9.3 offers a convenient means of analyzing the various types of industrial policy in relation to its precise focus and whether it is intended to be accelerative or decelerative. In box 1 lies the 'national champion' strategy. Here the state attempts through sponsoring mergers and financial aid to build up a major and internationally competitive enterprise. This sort of initiative was especially fashionable in the 1960s in Europe and led, for example, to the rise of the electrical giant Thomson in France and the motor goliath British Leyland in the United Kingdom. Many economists now argue that this policy, which involves the state in 'picking winners', is a high-risk strategy. Thomson remains dominant in France but out-competed by Japanese producers in world markets. British Leyland, despite continued doses of taxpayer funding through the 1970s and 1980s, by 1990 (renamed Rover) had shrunk to being a minor player in the European car market.

Box 2 includes industrial policy aimed at developing 'sunrise industries', usually taking advantage of new technologies, for example in computing, biotechnology and telecommunications. Once again it relies upon the ability of government to recognize where competitive advantage in the future will lie. The downside risk is the development of industries which can never compete against more efficient foreign rivals without state aid.

Turning to decelerative programmes, box 3 is the typical 'lame duck' strategy. An example might be the subsidies given in the 1970s to the Chrysler motor corporation in the United States when it was faced with financial collapse. In so far as the aim of a decelerative programme is to slow down for economic and social reasons the *pace of decline*, the policy might be defended, provided it does not impede necessary long-term restructuring. At the time of writing, Chrysler is again in difficulty having failed to stem the growth in market share in the United States of the Japanese motor manufacturers.

Lastly, box 4 is concerned with 'problem industries'. In Europe and North America since the 1970s large amounts of state aid in the form of subsidies or protection from imports have been directed at industries such as shipbuilding, steel, textiles and coal. As a result

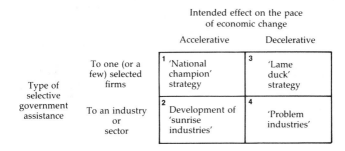

Figure 9.3 Basic types of industrial policy (Source: Based on J. Burton (1991) 'Industrial policy: the European context', *Business Studies*, Oct., p. 6)

the decline of these industries has been slowed down, though rarely reversed. State funding and restrictions on imports tend to create a dependence on continued protection against market forces. Too often decelerative industrial policies mask continued inefficiencies in the industry at a long-term cost to the public in terms of higher prices and slower economic growth. For example, 'temporary' taxpayer funding can turn into permanent protection as governments capitulate to the demands of politicians, whose constituencies would be adversely affected by industrial closures, and self-interested pressure groups, notably trade unions with members in the industries.

On the basis of this discussion, we can summarize the problems faced by industrial policy as follows:

- **Picking winners**. This is fraught with difficulty. Who in the 1960s accurately predicted the rise of microcomputers or the success of home video recorders and the compact disc player? In the main these products were developed by enterprises operating in highly competitive product markets, not by state-protected firms. Even when governments accurately pinpoint market opportunities, there is a clear danger that state aid will cushion inefficiencies in firms. Where this occurs development is fatally slowed down and costs of production are raised so that the firm can never be a major player in the world market.

- **Supporting losers**. Decelerative industrial policies may bring economic and social benefits to hard-pressed industries and regions, but past experience of this policy suggests that governments find it difficult to remove taxpayer support once granted. This has two effects. First, it slows to a trickle industrial restructuring. Resources remain tied up in lame duck firms and industries, when they could earn a higher return elsewhere. As a consequence economic growth is reduced. Secondly, it stimulates governments in other countries to protect their industries. For example, if cars exported from France benefit from state largesse to French manufacturers, they undermine the competitiveness of car producers in other countries. This leads to demands in those countries for matching state aid. The result is a 'beggar my neighbour' policy with taxpayers and car buyers the major losers.

Disillusionment with the longer-term economic effects of both accelerative and decelerative industrial policies led certain governments in the 1980s (notably in the United Kingdom) to pursue a different type of industrial policy. Instead of state interference with market forces, some governments have introduced programmes aimed at reducing state subsidies and controls, while re-introducing market competition into areas of the economy served by sleepy state monopolies. The main features of such programmes in the United Kingdom have been the following:

- **Liberalization of markets**. For example, opening up bus and coach services to competition.

- **Privatization**. The sale of nationalized industries to the private sector, e.g. the electricity, gas, telecommunications and water industries.

- **Competitive tendering**. Opening up certain state-supplied services, such as refuse collection and hospital cleaning, to private firms and introducing more competition in other areas of public procurement, notably defence contracts.

- **Reducing state subsidies**. The reduction or ending of state financing of both sunrise and lame duck firms.

- **Enterprise initiatives**. The redirection of state funding and other support towards retraining programmes and assisting the start-up of small enterprises.

As a result of these programmes, the nature of industrial intervention in the United Kingdom has been substantially altered away from a dependence upon state aid towards a much greater reliance on market forces. This has been copied in a number of other countries, both in the developed and developing world, and accords with the idea of a 'level playing field' for producers to compete internationally, not least in Europe.

The purpose of the EC is to provide a free trade area in Europe in which competition will not be distorted by state subsidies, tariffs and preferential procurement policies. In particular, Article 92 of the founding treaty, the Treaty of Rome, requires the eventual elimination of state aid which distorts competition. The move to a single market has added impetus to the ending of national subsidies to industry and the removal of preference for domestic suppliers when tendering for state contracts.

In recent years, the EC has been developing its own industrial policy aimed at developing sunrise industries. In particular, research and technical development, especially in the information technology, biotechnology, energy and telecommunications industries have been encouraged. Encapsulated in periodic Framework Plans, these programmes now exhaust around 4% of the EC's budget and the share is likely to grow. Alongside such initiatives the EC has not shunned intervention at the 'lame duck' level. For example, in the 1980s the EC 'planned' the reduction in European steel-making capacity and in 1991 agreed a European policy on Japanese car imports aimed at protecting EC producers until the end of the 1990s.

As in the case of macroeconomic policy, in the 1990s EC industrial policy is likely to become more important and national policy relatively less so. The major question to be addressed is the extent to which, in the face of political pressures, European industrial policy will drift towards 1970s style 'picking winners', putting it at odds with UK policy in the 1980s. Such an industrial policy would also conflict with the EC's activities in preserving healthy and competitive markets.

Competition law

The growth of large firms operating in oligopolistic or near-monopolistic markets has led governments to introduce competition laws. The case for state interference to promote competition comes directly from economic theory. As we saw in Chapter 4, a high degree of competition leads to the following benefits:

- Lower prices.
- A normal profit level.
- Lower costs of production.
- More consumer choice.

By contrast, monopolies and restrictive practices, where firms band together to agree production quotas and prices, imply high profit-making or inefficiency at the expense of the consumer.

The first laws of importance aimed at regulating monopolies and restrictive practices were introduced in the United States in 1890 and 1914. However, in Europe sympathy for the idea of economies of scale meant that similar legislation was delayed until after the Second World War. The United Kingdom passed legislation for the first time in 1948 when it established a Monopolies Commission (this was renamed the Monopolies and Mergers Commission in 1965 when its brief was extended to proposed mergers); but restrictive practices were not tackled until 1956 and only in 1976 was the Office of Fair Trading established at government level to oversee the operation of competition policy.

Today in most of the major economies firms with a dominant share of their market (broadly defined as 25% in the UK – other countries have their own definitions) can be subjected to investigation and fines imposed where abuse is discovered. Similarly, restrictive practices are either prohibited or severely regulated by national governments. In addition, however, firms in Europe are increasingly confronted by the requirements of European competition law. This law applies not only to companies based in the EC but potentially to any company operating in the EC, e.g. a Japanese company distributing goods to one or more EC markets. The Treaty of Rome includes the following two main Articles regulating competition:

- **Article 85**. This prohibits restrictive agreements and practices in so far as they 'affect trade between member-states' *and* restrict or distort competition. All agreements have to be notified to the EC and those relating to price fixing, market sharing, production quotas, discrimination between consumers, collective boycotts and tie-in clauses are specifically prohibited. An agreement may be exempted from the rigours of Article 85 only where it contributes 'to improving the production or distribution of goods or to promoting technical or economic progress' *and* it allows consumers 'a fair share of the resulting benefit'. Exemptions may be granted on an individual or a block basis. Block exemptions can be given for agreements relating to specialization, exclusive distribution, exclusive purchasing, patent licensing, R&D and motor vehicle distribution.

- **Article 86 of the Treaty of Rome**. This prohibits 'any abuse by one or more undertakings of a dominant position within the common market or a substantial part of it' in so far as it affects trade between member-states. A 'substantial part' has been interpreted as including any one of the major EC national markets, e.g. Germany or France. 'Dominance' has been defined as occurring where a firm has the power to behave to an appreciable extent independently of its competitors and customers.

European competition law is administered by Directorate General

IV of the European Commission which has considerable investiga-
tory powers. Whenever an infringement of the law is suspected, DG
IV may examine books and records, enter premises and question
management. It may also levy penalties for infringing the law of up
to 10% of a company's worldwide turnover. For example, in 1989
BPB Industries was fined more than 3 million ECUs for offering
fidelity payments to large customers in return for a promise not to
buy from French and Spanish competitors. In a further case, ICI was
fined 10 million ECUs for operating a cartel with other European
manufacturers of polypropylene; while more recently a price-fixing
arrangement relating to polyethylene resulted in penalties on the
companies involved totalling 60 million ECUs. In administering
European competition law, though subject to scrutiny by the full
European Commission, DG IV is effectively investigator, prosecutor,
judge and jury. The only appeal against an EC ruling is to the
European Court of Justice in Strasbourg.

In addition to monitoring the extent to which companies in
Europe conform to the requirements of Articles 85 and 86, DG IV
also intervenes where governments are felt to be unfairly subsidiz-
ing their own firms. Articles 92 to 94 of the Treaty of Rome state that
government aid which distorts or threatens to distort competition
and which affects trade within the EC is incompatible with the
common market. Thus the EC has recently required repayment of
French government support to the state-owned car maker Renault
and of some of the funding provided by the UK government to
smooth the sale of the Rover car company to British Aerospace. For
obvious reasons, however, DG IV has been more effective at
prosecuting companies for breaches of the competition rules than it
has been in pursuing offending member-governments!

Neither Article 85 nor Article 86 directly addresses the subject of
mergers. When the Treaty of Rome was drafted in the mid-1950s
mergers were far rarer than they are today, especially mergers
between companies operating in different EC countries. In the year
to June 1989, however, the European Commission recorded almost
500 mergers in the industrial sector alone with over a third involving
companies active in a number of EC markets.

In response to the trend towards EC-wide mergers in the run-up
to the establishment of the Single European Market, the EC
member-states agreed in September 1990 to extend European competition law to the control of mergers. For many years DG IV had
intervened where a European merger created a monopoly which
infringed Article 86, but the new powers mean that it can now
scrutinize and prevent mergers *before* dominance occurs. Mergers

covered by the new law include those involving companies with a combined turnover of more than 5 billion ECU, provided each company has sales in the EC of more than 250 million ECU. Thus the new EC law gives DG IV sole jurisdiction on mergers which have an important European dimension, though national governments can request the EC to transfer jurisdiction to them where a merger affects a distinct national market or where it threatens the public interest, e.g. mergers involving national media. Smaller mergers and takeovers, and those where all the companies involved have more than two-thirds of their sales in one member-country, will continue to be scrutinized only by member-countries' monopoly regulations.

Today firms operating in the EC need to take care that they do not infringe EC competition law. In the past governments have often turned a blind eye to the creation of national monopolies able to achieve economies of scale and so compete successfully in the international market. In the future this will not be so easy since most mergers of any size will have to satisfy the requirements of EC law over which national governments do not have discretion. Therefore, in Europe managerial decisions on restructuring are now increasingly constrained by the need to satisfy Articles 85 and 86. They can also be affected by European regional policy.

Regional policy

Ideally, to overcome imbalances in the development of different regions of an economy, labour would move from areas of over-supply to areas of labour shortage, attracted by higher wages. Similarly, capital would move in search of higher returns offered in regions in need of major capital investment. In other words, workers would move in search of work and businesses would move in search of cheaper labour. In practice, however, labour often lacks mobility because it does not have the required skills, or because of language and cultural barriers, family ties, housing costs and so on. Also, investment funds tend to go to those regions which are expanding quickly, where demand is buoyant therefore, and hence the expected rate of return is highest.

The result is an economic and social divide between the expanding regions with high per capita income growth and low unemployment, and the more depressed regions with lower purchasing power and high unemployment. Not only is this considered to be politically and socially undesirable, it also involves economic waste. For example, capital equipment, including social capital such as hospitals, schools and roads, may be under-utilized in areas of declining population, while expanding areas suffer increased congestion. Eventually, regional demand and supply pressures can spill over into higher national inflation as wages and prices are bid up in the areas of shortages.

Regional differences in economic performance in the United Kingdom and in certain other parts of Europe first came to prominence in the inter-war years as the old staple industries of the industrial revolution – coal, textiles, iron and steel, and shipbuilding – went into decline. This prompted governments to introduce measures aimed at alleviating the worst social and economic excesses of regional depression. After the Second World War regional policies were developed at the national level, but more recently there have been moves to develop a co-ordinated regional policy for the EC in response to marked variations in incomes throughout the Community.

Regional policy takes two broad forms as follows:

- **Reversing regional decline**. Governments have attempted to attract new industries into the relatively depressed regions by the use of government grants, relocation expenses, a preferential tax regime, providing business premises at subsidized rents, government factory building programmes, land reclamation and more lax planning regulations.

- **Limiting regional expansion**. Governments have limited the building of new factories and offices in areas of high growth in the hope that businesses would thus locate instead to the more depressed regions. Also, government departments have relocated activities to areas considered to be in need of development.

In the 1980s in the United Kingdom, consistent with its distrust of state intervention, the Conservative government reduced the scope of regional aid in an attempt to reduce its overall costs and to target it more productively. By 1979 the 'assisted areas' included over 40% of the UK working population, leading to criticism that regional aid was spread too thinly and perhaps too indiscriminately. Controls on setting up businesses in the prosperous south-east were abolished

and in 1988 the Regional Selective Assistance Scheme was introduced, which removed the automatic award of state aid in assisted
areas. At the same time, smaller and more focused areas such as
derelict land, especially in the inner cities, were identified for aid
and Urban Development Corporations were established. Between
1981 and 1991 regional assistance to depressed areas fell from
around £1.8 billion to just under £1.4 billion in 1990–1 prices. In
other countries there has been a similar reassessment of the benefits
of traditional regional policies.

Economists Moore, Rhodes and Tyler (1986) who studied the
operation of UK regional policy concluded that it had been beneficial
and had helped to create around 784,000 new jobs between 1960 and
1981. By contrast, critics of state aid to the regions, which include
free-market economists, argue that the policy is expensive and
unnecessary – market forces can solve the problem. They point to
evidence of labour and capital responding to price signals, for
example around 11,000 jobs relocated from high-cost London in 1990
alone. They also cite figures for foreign investment in the United
Kingdom. In the late 1980s this went disproportionately to the
regions where wages are lower. For example, between 1988 and
1990 Scotland with 8% of the UK GDP got 23% of inward
investment, while the south-east with 37% of GDP got only 4%.
These same critics of regional policy also cite the high level of
taxpayer subsidy that has traditionally been associated with regional
policy. In the 1960s and 1970s each job created by UK regional policy
is estimated to have cost the taxpayer around £35,000 (at 1984
prices). Critics of regional policy who object to the principle of state
involvement would prefer to see regional deprivation solved by
removing what they see as impediments to the mobility of labour
and capital, namely national wage bargaining, planning restrictions
which limit new factories and housing estates, and unemployment
and other welfare benefits.

As in the case of competition policy, the EC is taking a greater role
in regional development. Regional differences within the EC seem to
have increased in the 1980s, while the creation of a single market
and the prospect of monetary union, which would rule out for
member-countries devaluation of their exchange rates to gain competitive advantage, will probably further exacerbate regional differences in economic performance. Currently, the most prosperous
parts of the EC are largely within the area encompassed by the
'golden triangle' of Milan, London and Frankfurt. By contrast, all of
Portugal, most of Greece, Calabria in Italy and parts of Spain have
income per head of only around 60% of the EC average.

To even out European incomes EC aid is directed especially at the following:

- Declining rural areas.
- Long-term and youth unemployment (through training and retraining programmes).
- Areas of industrial decline (e.g. coal and steel areas).
- Regions designated as 'less developed', which include most of Southern Europe and Ireland.
- Investing in infrastructure schemes, e.g. roads and telecommunications, and promoting energy conservation in backward regions.

EC money must be additional to funds that the national government has already agreed to spend. Member-governments submit five-year development programmes detailing how the money is to be spent and regional and local authorities must be involved in the planning process. Regional funding is then allocated via national governments (in the United Kingdom it is channelled through the offices of the Department of Trade and Industry).

EC regional policy is administered by the Regional Directorate of the European Commission (DG XVI), which has around 300 staff. DG XVI oversees expenditure out of the European Regional Development Fund (ERDF) first established in 1975. At present EC money accounts for only around 15% of total regional spending in the EC, but current plans are for the Fund to double to around one-quarter of the EC budget (14.5 billion ECUs). Within the ERDF 'structural funds' have been allocated covering three broad areas: the regions, social needs and declining farming areas.

Concluding remarks

The previous chapters in this book have been primarily concerned with the firm's 'internal environment'. In other words, they are concerned with matters which managers can influence or control directly, notably demand, costs of production, employment levels, levels of investment and the 'marketing mix'. By comparison, the role of government may seem remote and uncontrollable. Yet governments today in *all* modern economies (and in many less advanced ones) intervene on a continuous basis in markets. Hence, they are just as significant to the firm's 'competitive environment' as competitors and suppliers. In Chapter 1 we introduced Michael Porter's notion of the five forces – the power of buyers, the power of suppliers, the threat from potential entrants, the threat from substitute products and actual rivalry in the market. It might be more useful, however, to think of the competitive environment in terms of a 'six-forces' model with government intervention being the influential sixth force. Recognition of the importance of government should trigger a search by firms to minimize the costs and to maximize the possible benefits of state intervention.

10

Business and economic forecasting

The essence of business and economic forecasting

In order to develop strategic plans and to respond effectively to changes in the economic environment, every business organization needs to have some idea as to the magnitude of its likely future sales. In Chapter 2 we introduced the concept of the demand function, which is concerned with the relationship between consumer demand for a good or service and a range of factors including own price, the price of complementary and/or substitute goods, consumers' expectations, population changes, etc. Firms that devote sufficient resources to derive the nature of the relationship between these factors and their future sales will be in a strong position to gain a significant competitive advantage in the market place over rivals who pay less attention to demand estimation. Of course there are many successful and profitable firms that employ few if any formal estimation procedures. However, in the complex world of business and commerce today there is clear evidence that the necessity for and popularity of formal estimation techniques is growing.

Understanding the nature of the market place and the reactions of consumers to changes in demand conditions is the first step towards effective forecasting of future sales and the development of a sound business plan. Business forecasting is, therefore, a critical management function – without 'good' forecasting the firm and its management are likely to miss important business opportunities. For example, forecasts of demand will be central to the decision of whether or not to build new production capacity; while decisions about whether to increase or decrease retail price may depend crucially on forecasts about raw material prices. Forecasting business and economic trends is, of course, not an exact science – if it was then no company would ever be taken by surprise and face the threat of unplanned closure! Nevertheless, there are well-established procedures available to management to eliminate as much guesswork as possible from business planning. These procedures, if followed methodically and correctly, should ensure that the final forecasts of sales and general economic indicators are more reliable than those based purely on intuition or hunch.

It is not possible to provide a comprehensive treatment of demand estimation and forecasting techniques in a single chapter; in particular, a detailed treatment of the appropriate mathematical techniques is well beyond the scope of this *Essence* book. Instead, the purpose of this chapter is to provide a broad overview of the subject, touching on most of the major aspects. It should lay the foundation for further study by the interested reader.

The subject of forecasting deals with the following issues:

- **Estimating demand relationships.** This is concerned with deriving the best specification of the demand function – that is, with *explaining* the relationship between the quantity of the product demanded by consumers and the factors that influence this demand. For example, how sales change as advertising expenditure increases based on actual past data on sales and advertising spend. Economists refer to this analysis as *interpolation*. This is the first key step towards forecasting demand and sales under changing conditions.

- **Forecasting demand.** Forecasting can form the basis of both short-term and long-term decisions. For example, a study of the pattern of sales for the past few weeks will help the firm to plan short-term production, inventory or advertising expenditure over the next few weeks. At the same time, demand estimation of a longer time span (many months and years) will enable the firm to determine the requirements for new production capacity, say, over the next decade, and to plan the development and introduction of new product lines and markets. Forecasting is thus concerned with the *extrapolation* or projection of future behaviour on the basis of past behaviour.

It will be appreciated therefore that demand estimation and forecasting, both in the short term and in the long term, can provide a useful basis for the strategic development of any business.

Collecting information on consumer behaviour

In general, demand estimation is concerned with the identification and measurement of the factors that jointly determine the demand for a firm's product(s). As we saw in Chapter 2, the most important determinants are likely to be included in the following list:

- The price of the good in question.
- The price of the good relative to the price of substitute and complementary goods.
- The level of advertising expenditure for the good.
- Income levels of potential buyers – who may be individuals, households or even other firms or the government (both at home and abroad).
- The cost and availability of finance (in terms of the rate of interest and credit terms available to potential customers).
- Changes in consumers' tastes and preferences and in their perception of the quality of the good relative to other goods.
- Consumers' expectations about future prices and the availability of the good.
- Changes in population in terms of age structure, growth, regional distributions, etc.

We also saw in Chapter 2 that we can estimate the responsiveness of demand for a product with respect to changes in its own price, i.e. the *price elasticity of demand*. This concept is not confined to own price changes but is applicable equally to any of the other determinants of demand listed above, such as income or advertising expenditure, as well as to changes in the prices of substitute or complementary goods. Such information about the relationship of the level of sales to each of these determining factors provides management with key data upon which to base production levels and to formulate strategy in terms of marketing, pricing, etc.

There are several methods available to help management collect information about consumer behaviour in relation to the firm's products and which form the basis of demand estimation and forecasting. These may be broadly categorized under the headings of *consumer surveys* and *market experiments*. Of course, the most common source of information is the historical record of sales collected by the firm itself about existing products. This will include details about sales levels, prices, advertising expenditure, production and design changes, etc., and anything else that may be thought to have an impact on consumer demand for the firm's products. This internal information may be augmented by information on external factors such as consumer income, the general level of retail prices, population changes, competitors' performance, credit conditions, etc., and any other external factors that may be thought to be relevant – including the weather conditions for example! (Details of the major sources of statistical information relevant to business are given in an Appendix to the book.) Before seeing how the information relating to these internal and external variables can be used statistically to estimate demand relationships it is useful to summarize the key features and limitations of consumer surveys and market experiments.

Consumer surveys

In essence, consumer surveys seek to discover the future buying intentions of consumers by eliciting their probable reactions to a range of conditions concerning price, advertising spend, product quality and design, and so on. The firm may carry out its own consumer interviews or it may commission a market research organization to conduct interviews on its behalf. For example, a random sample of consumers could be asked how much of the product they would buy if its price was reduced by 10%. This would help the firm to derive an estimate of the price elasticity of demand. The consumers could even be asked to state the current price of the product – if awareness of the actual price is low this might suggest that demand for the product is relatively price insensitive!

The major limitation of consumer surveys and of all such interview techniques is that the questions being asked are hypothetical – they are 'what if' scenarios. Answers to such questions may prove to be inaccurate in the sense that consumers may not *actually* behave in the manner indicated. A great deal of skill is required on the part of the institution conducting the survey to ensure that the questions are not misleading and that they are framed in such a way that the respondent is not enticed into giving the answer the firm wanted in the first place. In general, consumer surveys are likely to be better at providing qualitative information about general market reactions rather than the concrete quantitative data which are needed for statistical demand estimation.

Market experiments

Rather than pose hypothetical questions to potential customers, the firm may opt instead to carry out a direct market experiment in order to test buyers' reactions to actual changes introduced, while attempting so far as is possible to keep other market conditions fairly stable or under control. For example, the product in question may be offered at different prices or in a range of designs or packaging, while holding the background conditions as constant as possible, perhaps using a control group of buyers for which no corresponding change is made. Other controlled laboratory-type experiments could involve giving money to buyers and telling them to shop in a particular supermarket. By varying prices, design, shelf location, etc., the experimenter can analyze consumer behaviour in a controlled environment. In these ways, the firm can estimate price and income elasticities of demand for various buyer groups and product ranges.

The main drawback of such market experiments is that consumers participating in them know that their actions are being monitored. This may distort their normal buying patterns and hence invalidate the experiment. In addition, market experiments can be very expensive to set up and administer. The sample size must be sufficiently large to provide reliable results, increasing the costs still further. Against these drawbacks must be set the fact that a market experiment may be the only reliable source of demand information available to a firm intending to launch a new product. The experiment in this case is a trial run in a segment of the market which is regarded as representative of the whole market.

In general, the different methods of market experimentation employed by firms fall under one of the following three headings:

- Sales-wave research.
- Simulated store techniques.
- Test marketing.

We comment briefly on each method in turn.

Sales-wave research

This involves the selection of a group of consumers, supplying them initially with the product at no cost. Sometime later the same product is then re-offered to them for sale along with competitors' products at prices which can then be varied a number of times (this method is commonly employed in the soap powder industry with the results often used as part of an advertising campaign – provided the results are favourable to the firm!). This type of experiment enables the firm to assess the rate of repeat purchases and to estimate the impact of different competing brands. Attitudes to different packaging designs can also be monitored in this way.

Simulated store techniques

These techniques involve the establishment of a sample group of shoppers who are shown a number of advertising commercials for a range of products, including those for a new product to be launched by the firm, and then giving them some money to spend (or to keep!). Purchases of the new product and of competitors' products by the sample group can then be monitored. Discussions may be held with the customers to discuss their buying preferences with later follow-up interviews to find out if these preferences have changed.

Test marketing

This involves actually selling the product in a limited number of locations with different packaging and advertising campaigns in order to test market reaction. The scale of the test marketing may be fairly small, based in only a few shops, or it could be a full-scale experiment spread across many regions of the country.

Consumer surveys and direct market experiments are thus important sources of qualitative information concerning consumer reactions and can provide useful broad indications of the likely scale of demand. However, more 'scientific' techniques are available for demand estimation, the most important is based on *regression analysis*.

Statistical estimation of demand relationships

Using internal data relating to sales levels, prices, advertising expenditure, etc., and external data relating to the wider economic environment such as consumers' income, credit conditions, population changes, etc., it may be possible to estimate statistically the demand function for a product using the technique of regression analysis. The basic principles involved in using this technique are well-established and straightforward, although there are a number of important statistical problems involved in arriving at reliable estimates. A detailed treatment of these problems lies beyond the scope of this book but we shall deal later with one particular difficulty referred to as the *identification problem* (for a fuller account of regression analysis and the underlying statistical problems see *The Essence of Statistics for Business* by M. C. Fleming and J. G. Nellis, Chapter 10). It will be sufficient for our purposes here to outline the steps of regression analysis as follows. These are illustrated in Figure 10.1.

Step 1: identification of variables

Ultimately, this will be based on a combination of judgement, observation and economic theory, i.e. the demand function (Chapter 2). It involves identifying those factors which are likely to be the most important determinants of demand for the good in question. As the analysis proceeds, this list may be increased or reduced as we learn more about the impact of certain variables on consumer demand.

Step 2: compilation of data

A data set will need to be compiled for each of the variables which are expected to influence demand. Much of this data will be internal while other data will be external but may be readily available from public records including government statistical sources. Other data may have to be especially generated via customer surveys and market experimentation.

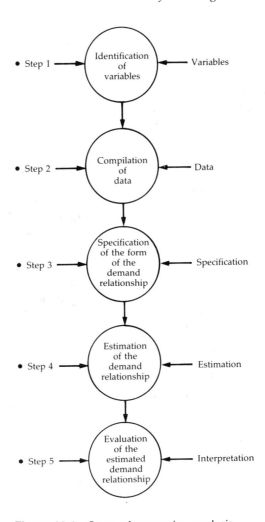

Figure 10.1 Steps of regression analysis

Step 3: specification of the form of the demand relationship

The nature of the relationship between the quantity of a good demanded and the variables which influence or determine this demand may not always be a simple one. The analyst will need to test various specifications of the relationship to discover the one which provides the best explanation or 'best fit'. The simplest and most common case is that of a linear relationship, such as:

$$Q = a + bP + cA + dY + e$$

where Q is the quantity of sales (referred to as the *dependent variable*), P is the price of the good in question, A is advertising expenditure and Y is real disposable income per head. The factors which affect Q are referred to as the *explanatory* or *independent* variables since they are intended to explain the observed variations in sales.

In this demand relationship, a, b, c and d are known as the *regression coefficients* and show by how much sales (Q) will change for a unit change in the associated independent variable, assuming all other independent variables are unchanged. For example, if b is estimated, using regression analysis, to equal $- 2.0$, then for every £1 increase in the price of the good, sales will fall by 2.0 units.

The last term, e, in the demand relationship is referred to as the *error term* and reflects the fact that the expression above is unlikely to explain fully all of the variation in sales. In other words, the e term captures the effect on sales of all the determinants that are not specifically included in the relationship. These might include irregular events such as strikes, severe winters, earthquakes, etc. as well as any errors in the input data sets. Demand estimation is not a perfect science – the world of business is never a certain one and hence the error term, e, reflects the proportion of the variation in sales that we have not been able to explain. Of course, as our knowledge of the market place increases and as the input data and demand estimation improve, the significance of the error term should decline.

The expression above assumes that sales are linearly related to the specified determinants. It may arise, however, that a more accurate expression for the relationship is in terms of a *multiplicative* or *exponential* form such that:

$$Q = aP^b A^c Y^d e$$

This form is commonly found in the estimation of relationships and has a number of advantages over the linear form. By taking logarithms of both sides of the expression we can convert this equation to one which is log-linear in form:

$$\log Q = \log a + b\log P + c\log A + d\log Y + \log e$$

The attractiveness of this form stems from the fact that we are now able to read off elasticity values directly: the estimated value for *b* now represents the price elasticity of demand, *c* represents the advertising elasticity of demand while *d* represents the income elasticity of demand. In the earlier linear case, these coefficients only measured the absolute (rather than proportional) change in sales for a unit change in *P*, *A* or *Y*.

Step 4: estimation of the demand relationship

The most commonly used procedure for estimating the demand relationship is known as the *method of least squares regression*. In essence, this enables us to find the values for the regression coefficients *a*, *b*, *c* and *d* defined above which give the best fit of sales (*Q*) to its determining variables (for example, *P*, *A* and *Y*). The method works by finding the values for the coefficients which minimize the sum of the squared positive and negative deviations of the actual (observed) sales values from those predicted by the fitted relationship. Figure 10.2 shows the principle of least squares regression for a simple case involving only one explanatory variable, say advertising, *A*. The relationship may be expressed as:

$$Q_t = a + cA_t + e_t$$

The subscript *t* refers to time and the relationship indicates that, for any particular time period *t*, sales (*Q*) are estimated to be positively related to the level of advertising expenditure (*A*) as shown in the figure. The estimated value for *a*, the intercept term, shows the level of sales suggested by this equation that would be achieved in the absence of any advertising (i.e. *A* = 0). The value of *a* is an indicator of the position of the graphed relationship while the value of *c* provides an estimate for the slope showing the effect of a change in the absolute value of advertising on the absolute volume of sales.

In this simple example, it is fairly easy to draw by eye the line passing through the actual plot of sales and advertising expenditure values which gives the 'best fit'. In most situations, however, there will be more than one explanatory variable – indeed there could be very many specified in the relationship – and hence we must use the technique of 'multiple' regression, rather than 'simple' regression. Conceptually, the least squares technique is the same in both cases though we cannot adequately show the relationship graphically.

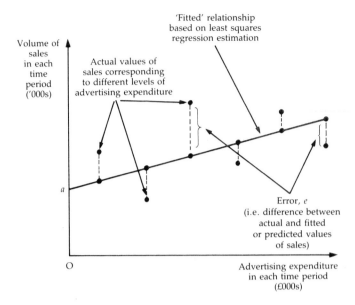

Figure 10.2   Regression of sales volume against advertising expenditure

Fortunately, a wide range of computer program packages are readily available which remove much of the physical effort from estimating the demand relationship. Indeed, there is little need for managers to even understand the mathematics involved though it is hoped that the brief discussion here has served to highlight the essence of the procedures.

Step 5: evaluation of the estimated demand relationship

Once the demand relationship has been specified and the estimates derived for the coefficients we then need to stand back and assess the plausibility of the results. Some of the questions to be asked are: Does the estimated relationship seem plausible? Does it contradict what has happened in the past? Is it in agreement with the relationships implied by economic theory? Above all, how reliable are the resulting statistical estimates?

Fortunately, most computer regression programs automatically produce a range of statistics which help us to evaluate the *reliability* of the estimated coefficients. Two particular statistics are especially important in this respect, namely the 'multiple correlation coefficient' and the 'standard error of the estimate'. The former measures the proportion of the total variation in the observed sales figures that is 'explained' by the estimated equation. It is thus an overall measure of the strength of the relationship between sales and the explanatory variables specified in the result. The latter allows us to attach a 'degree of confidence' to the estimated value of sales based on the regression equation. We can then state with, say, 95% confidence, that the actual sales level will fall within a certain range of variation around the estimated value of sales. It should be clear that the higher the value of the multiple correlation coefficient and the lower the value of the standard error of the estimate, then the more confidence we can have in our estimated demand function as an accurate representation of the true relationship between sales and the explanatory variables. In a similar way, from the 'standard errors' for each of the independent variables we are able to reach a view about the reliability of the predicted relationship between demand and each of the variables. For example, we can reach a view about whether the predicted relationship between advertising and sales is statistically significant.

The above discussion is intentionally only a very brief summary of regression analysis. Also the technique is not without problems and challenges for the analyst. We have already noted the requirement for adequate data on the relevant dependent and explanatory variables. This is the first major hurdle in demand estimation. Another problem which may arise involves the possibility that the explanatory variables themselves may be statistically correlated. The extent to which this problem exists – referred to as the *degree of multicollinearity* – will result in unreliable estimates of the coefficients for the individual explanatory variables. There are statistical techniques available for minimizing this problem but they are beyond the scope of this book.

In general, it is important to stress that the statistical estimation of demand relationships based on regression analysis does not provide an *exact* measure of the link between demand and its determinants. It simply shows the 'best-fitting' relationship – i.e. that which fits the existing data best! In some cases this best fit may in fact be very poor and hence of little value to management in estimating and forecasting the level of demand for the product.

A further problem, and one which we briefly referred to earlier, is known as the *identification problem*.

The identification problem

The simplest illustration of the identification problem arises when we attempt to relate the price of a good to its sales over time. For example, a manager given the task of estimating the demand curve for a particular product might, understandably, plot the quantity demanded in 1991 against the 1991 price, the quantity demanded in 1990 against the 1990 price and so on. If the resulting plot of points for 1989–91 were as shown in Figure 10.3, it would be tempting for the manager to conclude that the demand curve for the product is DD.

This approach, however, is seriously flawed for the market price at any point in time is determined by both the demand and supply curves, if the market is competitive. Specifically, the equilibrium value of price will be at a level where the demand and supply curves intersect, showing the quantity that consumers are willing to buy and suppliers are prepared to supply at that price. It is very likely that the demand and supply curves for the product will be different each year. For example, as shown in Figure 10.4, the supply curve may have shifted (from S_{89} in 1989 to S_{90} in 1990 and to S_{91} in 1991), representing a change over time in the underlying conditions of supply. In addition, the demand curve may also have shifted (from D_{89} to D_{90} to D_{91}) reflecting a change in the conditions of demand, e.g. a rise in incomes. If we superimpose the curve DD from Figure 10.3, it will be seen that this is not a good estimate of the demand

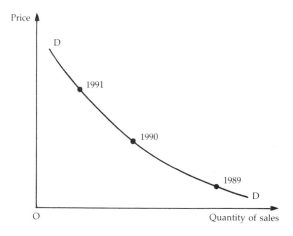

Figure 10.3 Plot of sales against price

curve for the product in *any* of the years, 1989 to 1991 (compare the slope of DD with the slopes of D_{89}, D_{90} and D_{91}). Thus there exists an identification problem in estimating the precise demand relationship.

The problem arises because of the need to hold constant the other non-price variables such as incomes, the prices of other goods, consumer tastes, advertising expenditure, etc. which affect demand, when constructing the demand curve. In practice, we cannot be sure that the demand relationship was constant during the period 1989–91. If the relationship had been fixed then, as the supply curve changed each year, we could be confident that DD does accurately represent the price/quantity demand relationship. As Figure 10.4 shows, shifts in the supply curve each year would map out various points on the demand curve.

This raises the problem of how to estimate a demand relationship if it has not remained fixed in the past. There are many solutions to this problem, some of which are simple and others which are very complex. Certain statistical techniques recognize that demand and supply quantities are determined simultaneously by price and that both of these curves shift in response to non-price variables. In essence, these techniques solve the identification problem by estimating a model of demand made up of a number of simultaneous equations, rather than a single equation.

Forecasting demand

So far we have discussed how firms can estimate the way in which consumer demand for their products responds to changes in price and other determinants. We have summarized how the causal link between the level of demand and its determinants may be quantified using regression analysis. However, in order to plan for production, inventory or advertising expenditure, in the short term and longer term, the firm must attempt to estimate future demand for its products – planning, therefore, necessitates *forecasting*. We now turn to describe those forecasting methods which are most commonly employed in business. At the outset it ought to be appreciated that all forecasting techniques should be treated with a degree of caution since none can be described as infallible. However, the fact remains that businesses (as well as governments) have

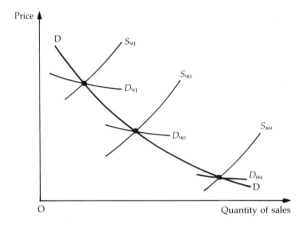

Figure 10.4 The identification problem

little choice but to make forecasts, albeit crude ones, in order to formulate decisions and future plans. Sometimes the forecasts arrived at will be implicit (based perhaps on 'know-how' and hunch) while at other times they will be explicit (based on some formal statistical techniques). The key challenge is to arrive at the best method for producing the best forecasts – 'best' ultimately can only be decided, of course, on the basis of comparing forecast and actual outcomes.

The various forecasting methods can be grouped conveniently under three headings, namely:

● Trend projection (or trend extrapolation).
● Leading indicators.
● Econometric modelling.

A fourth method, *survey analysis*, could be added to this list, but we have already covered this in our earlier discussion of demand estimation.

The choice of the most suitable method to be employed will depend on the answers to a number of questions relating to the forecasting problem at hand. The questions are as follows:

● **How far forward do we need to forecast?**
  A technique suitable for short-term projection may not be at all relevant for longer-term forecasting and planning.

- **What degree of accuracy is required in the forecasts?**
  Forecasting can be an expensive exercise and hence management must weigh up the cost of achieving greater accuracy against the additional benefit which they can expect to derive.

- **How quickly is the forecast needed?**
  Short-term forecasts, by definition, need to be derived quickly but they are likely to have only a short life span in the sense that they will quickly become outdated.

- **How accurate and complete are the underlying data which form the basis of the forecasts?**
  No forecasting technique can make up for inadequacies in the primary information available.

We now discuss each of the three forecasting methods listed above, keeping these questions to the fore.

Trend projection

The simplest type of forecasting method is a straightforward projection (or extrapolation) from the trend of past sales data. This is particularly useful when management is interested in arriving at short-term forecasts since it can reasonably be assumed that the behaviour of sales in the recent past will be a useful indicator of their behaviour in the near future (for example, the demand for bread in shops is unlikely to change significantly from one week to the next). In general, sales figures for most consumer goods tend to display stable behaviour over time.

Trend projection is not concerned with an explanation of *why* sales vary over time; we are not interested in estimating a demand relationship. Instead, the aim is more limited in that it is restricted simply to predicting the future volume of sales, without quantifying responsiveness to the various factors which determine demand. Since time and observations of past sales are the only variables to be used, the technique of trend projection is also frequently referred to as 'time series analysis'.

The simplest form of trend projection is illustrated in Figure 10.5, where the level of sales in recent time periods is represented by dots. The solid line provides the 'best fit' to these sales volumes, fitted by simple linear regression (as described earlier in this chapter) or simply by visual inspection. The broken line represents an extension of the sales trend into the future and is based solely on the assumption that the past trend will persist in the forthcoming

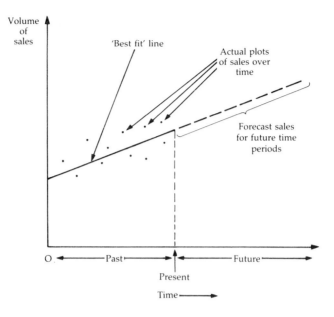

Figure 10.5 Trend projection forecasting

time periods. There is no attempt, therefore, to adjust the forecast to allow for a change in any of the causal factors which determine sales.

A more sophisticated approach to trend projection breaks down the time series of past sales data into four components (this is often referred to as the *decomposition method*). These components are as follows:

- **Trend (T).** This shows long-run changes in the data which result from fundamental developments in population, economic prosperity, technology, etc.
- **Seasonal variation (S).** During the year, demand for many products is likely to change with the seasons (for example, the demand for ice-cream in the summer and the demand for toys at Christmas).
- **Cyclical variation (C).** Sales and company performance may be subject to more or less regular fluctuations every few years, perhaps broadly in line with the general ups and downs of the wider economy or in the company's particular industry sector.

- **Random shocks (R)**. Sales may sometimes fluctuate as a result of random and unpredictable events such as floods, wars, strikes, etc. This component would also include any other irregular variation in sales which is unexplained in terms of any causal factor (this random variation might simply be due to a sudden change of consumer tastes, for no predictable reason!).

Figure 10.6 shows these components in terms of a hypothetical example based, say, on the sales of domestic electric cooling fans over a period of fifteen years. It can be seen that there is (a) a rising trend in sales perhaps associated with rising real income and a greater demand for comfort; (b) a seasonal pattern of demand with peaks in the summer and troughs in the winter (not surprisingly); (c) a cyclical pattern associated perhaps with the underlying per-formance of the economy in terms of growth and government economic management; and (d) irregular shocks arising from events such as oil crises, sudden interest rate surges, wars, etc. (the effect of these random shocks, while perhaps not obvious from the graph, is included as part of the otherwise unexplained variations in the short-term regular patterns).

As with regression analysis for demand estimation, many com-puter packages are available which break down time series data into

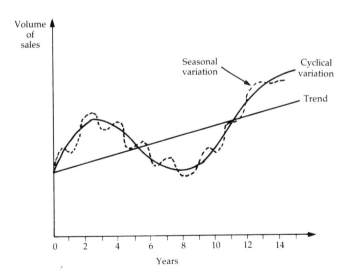

Figure 10.6 Decomposition of sales data over time

the above four components. There is little need, therefore, to elaborate further on the underlying technical procedures. It is worth noting, however, that different approaches to decomposition can be taken, depending on how one judges the four components to be related. Essentially, two choices are available. The components of the time series may be viewed as an *additive model* such that the sales data (Q) may be decomposed as:

$$Q = T + S + C + R$$

where T is the trend value of sales, S represents the seasonal variation component of sales, C the cyclical variation and R the random shocks. Alternatively, the relationship may be stated in terms of a *multiplicative model* whereby:

$$Q = T \times S \times C \times R$$

A number of statistical procedures can be used to check the appropriateness of the model chosen and to improve further the quality of the forecasts made based on the decomposition method. For example, quite simply the accuracy can be checked by 'back-forecasting'. This involves using the model to estimate demand for an earlier period for which actual sales data are available and checking the estimated against the actual figure.

Leading indicators

Another common approach to planning used by business economists is to try to discover any correlation between sales and other economic variables over time. There are many examples where movements in two or more economic variables are closely associated, with changes in one variable being followed more or less consistently by changes in the other. For example, as real disposable income rises generally in the economy, the demand for most consumer goods eventually increases, the time lag being longer perhaps for the more expensive items such as durables and shorter perhaps for items such as clothing. It is therefore extremely helpful to management if a variable or group of variables can be found whose time series leads the sales figures for the firm's products. Information about such variables, referred to as *leading indicators*, is a great aid to demand forecasting.

Most governments devote a great deal of effort to analyzing the behaviour of a wide range of economic variables over a long period of time. The aim is to find out whether each economic indicator turns downwards before, at, or after the peak of a business cycle, and whether it turns up before, at, or after the trough. Variables that go down before the peak and up before the trough are called *leading indicators*; variables that go down at the peak and up at the trough are called *coincident indicators*, while variables that go down after the peak and up after the trough are referred to as *lagging indicators*.

Some examples of leading indicators used in the United Kingdom and United States in forecasting trends in the economy are the following:

- New housing starts.
- Stock Exchange indices.
- Price to unit labour cost ratios.
- New orders for durable goods.
- Orders for new plant and equipment.
- Changes in manufacturing stocks.
- Changes in consumer credit.
- New orders for machine tools.

These variables tend to turn upwards before an economic trough is reached in anticipation of a future recovery, while they also tend to slow down in advance of a peak in expectation of a subsequent downturn. Similarly, coincident indicators often include corporate profits, gross domestic product, and employment while lagging indicators may include unemployment levels, retail sales, personal incomes and retail prices (since inflationary pressures can be slow to respond to a general economic downturn).

The use of leading indicators as a sales forecasting technique is applicable mainly to short- and medium-term forecasts. This is because there may only be a relatively short time lag (say, a few months) between a change in the leading indicator and a corresponding movement in sales. Moreover, management may be reluctant to rely too heavily on this method for longer-term forecasting since it does not provide an explanation for sales, but merely helps to identify turning points in the direction of movements of sales. The method is also unable to indicate the magnitude and exact timing of any subsequent change in sales. However, the method is an inexpensive one – very often, the leading indicator information will be published by the government statistical office!

Econometric modelling

We have already described how econometric modelling can be used to estimate demand relationships. Once this relationship has been specified it can be used as a tool for estimating future demand by including forecast values for the determining variables. For example, it will be recalled that sales (Q) were estimated as a function of price (P), advertising expenditure (A) and disposable income per head (Y), such that:

$$Q = a + bP + cA + dY$$

The error term, e, is not included explicitly here since any error will be reflected in the accuracy of the forecast itself when compared with the actual outcome. Forecasts for Y will be available from the government statistical office, while forecasts for P and A will be available from the firm itself since the firm controls these variables (note that earlier we stated the equilibrium price is determined by demand and supply; of course, there is nothing to stop the firm setting whatever price it likes but it will have to accept whatever demand arises at that price – it cannot control price and demand independently). The forecasts for P, A and Y will therefore provide a basis for forecasting sales (Q) from the demand relationship.

The above example is a fairly trivial one, involving only a single demand equation. In reality, multi-equation models are likely to be necessary involving a great number of determining variables and complex mathematical manipulations. The principles, however, are the same and, fortunately for management, the job of econometric modelling is usually left to specialist economists and statisticians.

Many multi-equation models are used by a number of government and private sector organizations in the United Kingdom. The most well-known of these are HM Treasury, the London Business School and the National Institute for Economic and Social Research, though many more are commonly cited in the press and academic literature. These models contain hundreds of equations variously intended to explain the level of expenditure by households, business investment expenditure, national output and employment, wages, retail and wholesales prices, interest rates, construction activity, etc. Like all forecasts, however, the reports issued by these well-known institutions are far from perfect. In recent years they have all attracted considerable criticism, especially from business, because of inaccuracies in some of their forecasts (with the benefit of hindsight of course!). Nevertheless, in the absence of a superior alternative, forecasts from econometric models such as these continue to be widely used by business and government as the basis for discussing future policy.

Econometric modelling has an important advantage over the other two forecasting methods outlined above. An attempt is made to account for future sales in terms of causal relationships using anticipated future values of those factors that are believed to affect demand. A more detailed understanding of 'cause and effect' helps management to accommodate changes in assumptions about future events in a more systematic way. This in turn facilitates the development of a range of scenarios and the formulation of appropriate business responses. In addition, the forecaster has the opportunity to improve the accuracy of the forecasts as time passes by adding new, up-to-date information into the forecasting model – there is, therefore, a learning curve. At the same time, however, it is important to recognize the danger of using econometric models simply as 'number crunching' devices – i.e. churning out forecasts under a vast spectrum of scenarios (some realistic, some fanciful, some bizarre!), especially since it is not very difficult to produce endless forecasts using today's computerized technology. It is vital that forecasting models are carefully and methodically constructed, representing a sound blend of economic theory with modern statistical methods.

Concluding remarks

In this chapter we have described the fundamentals of demand estimation and forecasting. From even the elementary treatment of the subject presented here, it will be clear that forecasting is one of the most challenging aspects of business analysis. It is also an area of business which, in recent years, has grown dramatically in importance as competition has grown both domestically and globally. The reader should not, however, be daunted by the technical aspects of forecasting, some of which we have only touched upon here. The advent of user-friendly personal computers has circumvented the mysteries of the 'statistician's black-box'. Nowadays, there is little need for managers to be fully conversant with the underlying technical aspects of forecasts. More important is the ability to interpret computer-generated results correctly with this interpretation complemented by good judgement and sound managerial experience. A degree of scepticism about all forecasts is, in fact, useful. It helps to avoid the danger of placing undue emphasis on hard, cold numbers which should represent only one component of management decision-making.

11

Business economics – a check list for managers

This book has been concerned with investigating various aspects of business economics and has highlighted the importance of an understanding of business economics in the preparation and development of an effective business strategy.

To stay ahead of the competition and to anticipate and react effectively to changes in markets requires an understanding of the forces of demand and supply and their impact on optimal prices and outputs in different market environments. In particular, firms operating in markets where competition is imperfect (hence having less elastic demand curves) typically have far more discretion over prices and outputs than firms operating in highly competitive markets. This suggests a strategy of product differentiation as an obvious option. The alternative, supplying undifferentiated products (products with high cross-price elasticities with substitutes), implies a need to be the low-cost producer since competition will centre on price, as emphasized by the perfect competition model. In addition, as we have seen, the precise response to market signals in terms of the price–output strategy adopted is dictated by the objectives of management – what goal or goals are being pursued? A firm that is intent upon maximizing short-term profit will pursue a different price and output configuration than, for example, a firm more concerned with maximizing sales revenue. This led on to a discussion of pricing strategies where it was observed that, as price is only one of a number of factors likely to determine consumer demand, attention should be paid to the complete 'marketing mix'. In turn management should not lose sight of the importance of sound investment appraisal when adjusting capacity to meet changes in demand, an issue explored in Chapter 7.

We concluded our review of business economics with a discussion of the labour market, the role of government in the economy and the subject of business and economic forecasting. The labour market cannot be ignored because labour costs frequently represent a large proportion of operating costs; while governments today play a central role in determining the economic environment in which businesses operate. Government policy can make or break the best planned and executed business strategy. Lastly, our approach to the subject of business forecasting was premised on the belief that when walking through a tunnel it is better to have at least partial light rather than complete darkness. In other words, in business some knowledge of likely future trends, for example in sales, and hence some knowledge of the relationship between demand and the factors impacting on demand, is superior to complete ignorance (or indifference) to the future.

We conclude this overview of business economics with a check list drawn from the principles explored in the book. The list provides a brief summary of the key topics discussed in the earlier chapters. But the main purpose of the list is to allow busy managers speedily to review their knowledge of their firm's economic environment, both internal and external, with a view to identifying the degree of competitive advantage (or disadvantage!) which exists and so as to identify those areas where more knowledge or information is needed. The list is presented as a series of key economic questions and is summarized in Figure 11.1 as a 'wheel of fortune'!

Check list for business success

Understanding the business objectives

- What are my objectives for each of the products, e.g. short-term profit maximization (using products as 'cash cows'), sales maximization (increasing market share), etc.?
- Are current product prices set at a level to achieve the desired objective?

- Is my competitive strategy primarily focused on being the low-cost producer or does it rely more on product differentiation? If my products are 'stuck in the middle', what action might be taken to change the product focus and how might rivals react?

Understanding the competitive market

- In what types of markets do I operate (highly competitive, monopolistic, etc.) and what are the implications for longer-term prices and profits?
- How do my main competitors set their prices and determine their expenditure on other aspects of the 'marketing mix'?
- Is there a threat from new competition? What barriers to entry into my markets exist and can be legally reinforced? Do I understand the limitations imposed by domestic and international competition law?
- What does new competition imply for my competitive position over the longer term?
- How might I best respond to changes in the market by altering the 'marketing mix' for my products?

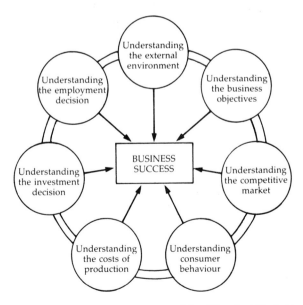

Figure 11.1 Business success – The Wheel of Fortune

Understanding consumer behaviour

- Do I know how different market factors affect the demand for my products and hence do I know (even in general terms) the demand function for each of my products?
- Is it likely that my prices will have to be changed in the immediate future and if so what are the own price elasticities of the products?
- Are the prices of substitute and complementary products likely to change and if so what are the relevant cross-price elasticities with my products?
- What is the income elasticity of demand for my products and what is the forecast for income changes in the next few years?
- Is it possible and would it be useful to have an economist estimate the demand coefficients for my products?
- Is price set mainly with a view to consumer demand or mainly with a view to covering supply costs (e.g. a 'cost-plus' pricing policy)? Is this consistent with my business objective?

Understanding the costs of production

- How elastic is the supply of each of the products I produce and hence how fast could I respond to changes in demand?
- How might supply elasticity be increased?
- What is the current marginal cost for each of my products and is it rising or falling and why? What does this mean for future competitiveness?
- Is there evidence of diminishing returns given current plant size and what does this imply for the investment programme?
- Am I getting the maximum economies of scale in production, and if not why not? What does this mean for my competitive position?

Understanding the investment decision

- Are discounted cash flow estimates consistently used in investment appraisal?
- Am I fully aware of available regional and other government financial incentives?
- Do I calculate the internal rate of return?

- What is the opportunity cost of capital investment – alternative business investment opportunities or a risk-free return in a bank account?
- Are *all* costs and benefits (internal and external) taken into consideration in investment appraisal?
- On what basis is the cost of capital calculated?

Understanding the employment decision

- Do decisions on employment take into account the marginal revenue product (i.e. the added value) of labour?
- Are wages set with regard to any rational economic criteria?
- What factors determine the supply of labour to the business?
- What are the implications for labour supply of current demographic trends?
- What action is being taken to anticipate unfavourable movements in labour costs?
- Are current wage differentials economically justified?

Understanding the external environment

- Is there a regular briefing in my company concerned with developments in the macroeconomic environment and related government policy and their likely impact on the business?
- Do I know what would be the demand for my products if interest rates rose or fell, or if the exchange rate depreciated or appreciated, or if there was a change in the rate of growth of consumer spending or investment?
- In developing business plans do I make use of any macroeconomic forecasts prepared by the various forecasting bodies, e.g. HM Treasury, London Business School, etc.?
- Are there any likely changes in the political, economic, social and technological (PEST) environment which will impact on my business?
- How should I respond to these events?

The above list is not intended to be exhaustive – indeed, it could not be exhaustive since what is important to one business may not be important to another. It is simply intended to provide a *basis* for identifying those economic factors which impact on the reader's business with a view to provoking a search for the relevant answers.

Business economics is best viewed as a tool kit for analyzing competition and market behaviour. Economists can provide insights though rarely precise answers. It is ultimately the manager who has to take the difficult decisions of business on a day-to-day basis and after weighing up the alternatives. Hopefully, however, this book will have assisted managers in understanding the challenges they face in the competitive economic environment in which they function and hence will have contributed to sounder decision-making.

Appendix:
sources of business
economics data
for managers

This appendix gives details of the principal sources of UK business economics data as well as the key international sources of data. The UK data are categorized according to the following headings:

1. General.
2. Economic growth.
3. Personal income and saving.
4. Industry and commerce.
5. Labour statistics.
6. Finance and inflation.
7. Foreign trade.
8. Non-official sources.

Two useful guides to UK statistical sources are available:

1. *Government Statistics: A brief guide to sources* (London: Information Services Division, Cabinet Office) (free).
2. CSO, *Guide to Official Statistics* (London: HMSO, occasional).

UK sources

1. General

Annual Abstract of Statistics, HMSO.
Bank of England Quarterly Bulletin, Bank of England.
Economic Briefing, HM Treasury. Monthly.
Economic Trends, HMSO. Monthly and annual supplement.
Financial Statistics, HMSO. Monthly.
Monthly Digest of Statistics, HMSO.
UK National Accounts, HMSO. Annually.
Regional Trends, HMSO. Annually.
Social Trends, HMSO. Annually.

2. Economic growth

Economic Trends, tables 6, 8, 26, 28, 68–71. Special section January, April, July and October.
Monthly Digest of Statistics, tables 1.1–1.3, 7.1.
UK National Accounts, sections 1–3.

3. Personal income and saving

Economic Trends, tables 10, 12, 14.
Financial Statistics, section 9.
Monthly Digest of Statistics, tables 1.5, 14.1, 14.2.
UK National Accounts, section 4.

4. Industry and commerce

Business Monitor MA3, Business Statistics Office. Annually.
Economic Trends, tables 16, 18, 22, 60, 62.
Financial Statistics, section 8.
Monthly Digest of Statistics, tables 1.7–1.9.
UK National Accounts, section 5.
Digest of UK Energy Statistics. Annually.
Transport Statistics Great Britain. Annually.

5. Labour statistics

Economic Trends, tables 34, 36, 38, 40.
Employment Gazette, HMSO. Monthly.
New Earnings Survey, HMSO. Annually.
Monthly Digest of Statistics, section 3.

6. Finance and inflation

Economic Trends, tables 5, 42, 52–66.
Employment Gazette, tables 6.1–6.7.
Family Expenditure Survey, Department of Employment, HMSO.
  Annually.
Financial Statistics. Monthly.
Monthly Digest of Statistics, tables 18.1–18.6.

Price Index Numbers for Current Cost Accounting, HMSO (annually).
Business Monitor MM17, HMSO (monthly) for producer price indices.

Financial Statistics, sections 3, 6, 7, 11.

Bank of England Quarterly Bulletin, Statistical annex.

7. Foreign trade

Overseas Trade Statistics of the United Kingdom, HMSO. Monthly
  and annually.

8. Non-official sources

British Institute of Management, London.
The Economist Intelligence Unit, London.
The Institute of Directors, London.
Cambridge Economic Forecasting, Cambridge.
The Confederation of British Industries, London.

International sources

General

UN Statistical Year Book and *UN National Accounts Statistics*, United Nations (UN), New York. Annually.
Yearbook of Labour Statistics, International Labour Organization (ILO), Geneva. Annually.
International Financial Statistics, International Monetary Fund (IMF), Washington. Monthly.
National Accounts, Organization for Economic Co-operation and Development (OECD), Paris. Annually.

EC

A wide range of statistics publications is published by the Statistical Office of the European Communities (SOEC) in Luxembourg. Selected titles are given below:

Basic Statistics of the Community. Annually.
Industry: Statistical yearbook.
Industrial Trends: Monthly statistics.
Industrial Production: Quarterly statistics.
Structure and Activity of Industry. Annually.
Earnings: Industry and services. Half-yearly.
Labour Force Survey. Annually.
National Accounts, 3 volumes. Annually.
External Trade: Statistical yearbook. Annually.

A full listing of EC statistical sources is available in *Eurostat Catalogue*, free from Eurostat and from the Office of Official Publications of the European Communities, Luxembourg. The European Communities Information Office can be contacted at 20 Kensington Palace Gardens, London W8 4QQ.

Other

Details of data sources can usually be obtained by contacting the appropriate Ministry of Trade or Finance or central bank.

References for further reading

There are many books which provide further in-depth treatment of the aspects of business economics covered in this book. Most, however, are aimed at the specialist student of economics, tailored to suit the needs of undergraduate degree courses. The following references have been selected because they build upon the contents of this book yet are intelligible to the non-specialist manager.

Brealey, R. A. and Myers, S. C. (1990) *Principles of Corporate Finance*, New York: McGraw-Hill International.

Call, S. T. and Holahan, W. L. (1984) *Managerial Economics*, Belmont, CA: Wadsworth Publishing Company.

Clarke, R. and McGuinness, T. (eds) (1987) *The Economics of the Firm*, Oxford: Basil Blackwell.

Crowson, P. (1985) *Economics for Managers: A professionals' guide*, London: Macmillan.

Davies, H. (1991) *Managerial Economics for Business, Management and Accounting*, Second Edition, London: Pitman.

Douglas, E. J. (1987) *Managerial Economics: Analysis and strategy*, Third Edition, Englewood Cliffs, NJ: Prentice Hall.

Ferguson, P. R. (1988) *Industrial Economics: Issues and perspectives*, London: Macmillan.

Hill, S. (1989) *Managerial Economics: The analysis of business decisions*, London: Macmillan.

Mansfield, E. (1990) *Managerial Economics: Theory applications and cases*, New York: Norton.

Moore, B., Rhodes, J. and Tyler, P. (1986) *The Effects of Government Regional Economic Policy*, London: HMSO.

Porter, M. E. (1985) *Competitive Advantage: Creating and sustaining superior performance*, New York: Free Press.

Reekie, D. W. and Crook, J. N. (1987) *Managerial Economics*, Third Edition, Oxford: Philip Allan.

Reekie, D. W. (1989) *Industrial Economics: A critical introduction to corporate enterprise in Europe and America*, Aldershot: Edward Elgar.

Robertson, D. H. and Dennison, S. (1960) *The Control of Industry*, Cambridge Economic Handbook, Nisbet, Cambridge: Cambridge University Press.

Index